FINGERTIP FACTS
for the
1955 CHEVROLET

First published in 1994 by Motorbooks International Publishers
& Wholesalers, PO Box 2, 729 Prospect Avenue, Osceola, WI
54020 USA

Motorbooks International is a certified trademark, registered
with the United States Patent Office

The information in this book is true and complete to the best of
our knowledge. All recommendations are made without any
guarantee on the part of the author or Publisher, who also
disclaim any liability incurred in connection with the use of this
data or specific details

We recognize that some words, model names and designations,
for example, mentioned herein are the property of the
trademark holder. We use them for identification purposes only.
This is not an official publication

Motorbooks International books are also available at discounts
in bulk quantity for industrial or sales-promotional use. For
details write to Special Sales Manager at the Publisher's address

Library of Congress Cataloging-in-Publication Data
Fingertip facts for the 1955 Chevrolet / Damon Enterprises.
    p. cm.
  ISBN 0-87938-850-1
   1. Chevrolet automobile—Specifications.   2. Chevrolet
automobile—History.   3. 1955 Chevrolet.   I. Damon
Enterprises.
   TL215.C48F56 1994
   629.222'2—dc20   93-33475

Printed and bound in the United States of America

THE NEW '55 CHEVROLET

More than a new car . . . . A NEW CONCEPT!

The Motoramic Chevrolet is more than a new car. It's a completely new concept of low-cost motoring—without parallel in automotive history.

Starting with a clean slate, Chevrolet first found out, through exhaustive research, exactly what people want in a car of lowest cost; then developed—in one compact design—values that exceed people's greatest expectations of a car of Chevrolet's class.

Fully three years were spent in this development—by an army of stylists, engineers, scientists, and technical experts. Only the best of many designs for each feature were considered—and then were developed and redeveloped, and tested and tested again to assure a superior car that would perform exceptionally well for a long, long time.

- NEW "Show Car" Styling
- NEW Coloramic Interiors
- NEW Body by Fisher
- NEW Box-Girder Frame
- NEW Sweep-Sight Wind-
  shield
- NEW Four-Fender Visibility
- NEW High-Level Air Intake
- NEW Air Conditioning
- NEW Glide-Ride Front
  Suspension

As the result, the new Motoramic Chevrolet is by far the most beautiful, most enjoyable, and finest performing Chevrolet ever built. Its lower silhouette makes the car look longer although its actual length is hardly changed; yet, inside, there is more room than ever. With dead weight pared to the bone, and power greatly increased, the car accelerates, follows the road, and climbs hills with amazing briskness. In comfort, safety, riding qualities, handling ease, responsiveness, and all-round roadability, it surpasses all of Chevrolet's high standards of the past and stands out as the most brilliantly conceived car in its field. Still, for all its exciting newness, it retains certain traditional Chevrolet values: down-to-earth dependability, exceptional economy of operation and upkeep, and highest quality at lowest cost.

Only Chevrolet, with its enormous resources, highest volume production, and great savings through mass manufacturing and mass purchasing, could conceive such a car as the Motoramic Chevrolet—

and only Chevrolet could achieve such a marvelous and outstanding result.

All the features of the Motoramic Chevrolet are described in this book. In addition to general sections which pertain to the car as a whole, separate sections are devoted to those features which contribute most to Style, Comfort, Structure, Ride, Engines, Power Teams and Controls. Each of these sections is complete in itself in that it considers not only those features which are standard but also those that are available at extra cost in the forms of accessories and optional equipment. For quick reference, the first page of each of these sections lists all the features described in the section and together, these first pages provide a complete list of the new car's features. The table of contents, on page 4 tells somewhat about the subjects covered in both general and feature sections; while a complete cross-reference index is provided at the end of the book.

CONTENTS

**THIS IS CONFIDENTIAL INFORMATION
FOR CHEVROLET SALES PERSONNEL ONLY.**

- A Brilliant Array of 14 Beautiful Models . . . a Model for Every Purse and Purpose.

- Three Great Series . . . Each with Distinctive Characteristics.

- Three 4-Door Sedans . . . One in Each Series.

- Three 2-Door Sedans . . . One in Each Series.

- The Glamorous Bel Air Sport Coupe.

- The Bel Air Convertible . . . for the Young in Spirit.

- The "Two-Ten" Delray Club Coupe . . . with Full Sedan Roominess.

- The Practical "One-Fifty" Utility Sedan.

- Two 4-Door Station Wagons . . . The Beauville, Newest Addition to the Bel Air Line, and the Ultra-Smart "Two-Ten" Townsman.

- Two 2-Door Station Wagons . . . The Sleek "Two-Ten" Handyman and its Companion in the "One-Fifty" Series.

- 190 Exciting Model-Color Selections.

- A Full Complement of Standard Equipment for Every Model.

- A Wonderful Selection of Equipment for Individualizing the Car.

- Power Assists of Every Kind . . . for Motoring at Its Best.

**MORE THAN A NEW CAR . . .
A NEW CONCEPT OF LOW-COST MOTORING!**

14 BEAUTIFUL MODELS

SERIES	SEDANS				SPORT MODELS		STATION WAGONS	
	4-DOOR SEDANS	2-DOOR SEDANS	CLUB COUPE	UTILITY SEDAN	SPORT COUPE	CONVERTIBLE	4-DOOR STATION WAGONS	2-DOOR STATION WAGONS
"ONE-FIFTY"	 Model 1503	 Model 1502		 Model 1512				 Model 1529
"TWO-TEN"	 Model 2103	 Model 2102	 Model 2124				 Model 2109	 Model 2129
BEL AIR	 Model 2403	 Model 2402			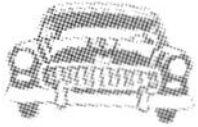 Model 2454	 Model 2434		Model 2409

A CHEVROLET FOR EVERY PURSE AND PURPOSE

The Motoramic Chevrolet is offered in 14 beautiful models in three series . . . every model is offered in a variety of color selections, a choice of optional and accessory equipment, plus a wide range of power teams —so that anyone can buy a Chevrolet that truly suits his desires, needs and budget.

BODIES

FOR EVERY PURPOSE

Chevrolet bodies—all by Fisher—may be grouped in three classes: the sedans, the sport models, and the station wagons.

The sedans are all made from the same basic design, with the same size passenger compartment and trunk. The four-door sedans provide direct access to both front and rear seats. The two-door sedans provide ease of entry to the front seat, through extra-wide doors, while access to the rear seat is facilitated by front-seat back rests that tilt inward as they are folded forward. The Utility Sedan is a two-door sedan in which a luggage compartment is provided instead of a rear seat; the Club Coupe provides full sedan roominess with special appointments and an all-vinyl interior.

Sport models include the Sport Coupe and the Convertible. The basic body for these models has a lower top and a longer rear deck than sedan bodies, to give the extra-long, low raciness so desired in fun cars.

The Sport Coupe features hardtop styling—the airiness of open sides with the security of a solid steel top; the Convertible has an automatically folding fabric top. Otherwise these two models are like the two-door sedans in that they have extra-wide doors and center-fold front seat back rests.

The basic body of the station wagons features a large load compartment behind the two seats, a rear seat that folds level with the load platform to enlarge the compartment, a spare wheel-well below the platform, tail- and lift-gates in the rear, and unique wraparound rear quarter windows. The two-door station wagons, like the two-door sedans, have extra-large doors and center-fold front-seat back rests; the four-door models offer direct access to both front and rear seats and the convenience of curbside loading.

For safety, every Chevrolet body is of all-steel construction, every Chevrolet door is hinged at the front, and every Chevrolet window pane is high quality safety glass.

MODELS

FOR EVERY PURSE

The Motoramic Chevrolet is offered in three series so that anyone can choose a model that fits his budget.

In the thrifty "One-Fifty" series, there is the choice of four-door sedan, two-door sedan, Utility Sedan, and two-door station wagon models. These are all full-size cars—practical, smart, and complete with every item that is needed for years of satisfying service.

In the de luxe "Two-Ten" series, there is a choice of four-door and two-door sedans,

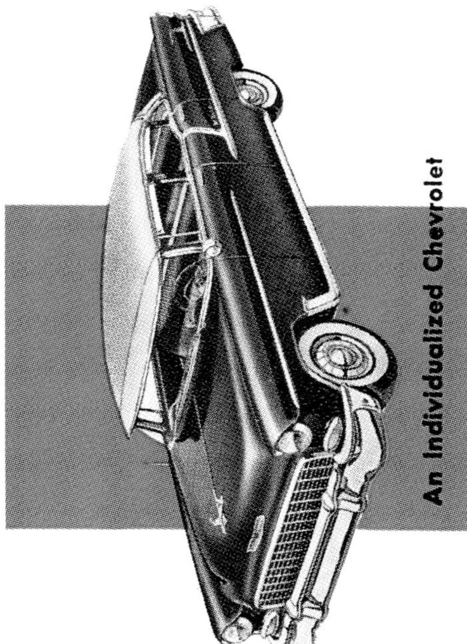

two station wagons and a Club Coupe. Sparkling chrome moldings added at the windows
and on the sides smarten the exteriors of
these models while the interiors are enhanced
with fine fabrics, color-keyed to the exteriors,
and such extra appointments as ash receptacles and arm rests.

In the luxurious Bel Air series, there is
the choice of four-door and two-door sedans,
the Sport Coupe, the Convertible, and the
Beauville four-door station wagon. These
are the glamour cars of the low-price field,
with distinctive exteriors and interiors that
rival the costliest cars in materials, appointments, and appearance.

All these models are complete in them-
selves, but for the person who wishes to
individualize his car, Chevrolet offers a full
line of accessories and optional equipment:
chrome, in useful items, to enhance the exterior; seat covers to enhance the interior;
radios, heaters, air conditioner, and many
other options that give him the same com-
forts and conveniences that he is used to in
his home—and, for ultra convenience, such
items as a power-positioned front seat and
power-controlled windows.

COLORS

FOR EVERY TASTE

All the colors of the rainbow! Yes, 190 different model-color combinations are offered in the Motoramic Chevrolet. Smart, modern pastel shades, gleaming dark tones, rich metallics—solids, two-tones, and a special two-tone color styling that inspires envious admiration. And all these colors are in highest quality, lustrous lacquer, applied in Chevrolet's famous "nine-step" finishing process that assures years and years of sparkling beauty.

AND POWER

FOR EVERY KIND OF DRIVING

Every Motoramic Chevrolet has the same basic chassis (frame, springs, wheels, and tires) designed to give a new concept of driving comfort. But for ease of control and performance that ranges from sparkling to spectacular, Chevrolet offers every selection of control and driving equipment that can be obtained in any car: standard steering or *power* steering, standard braking or *power* braking, standard driving, standard driving plus overdrive, or *Powerglide* automatic driving—with either a Six or V8 engine—in six different *power* teams:

TRANSMISSION	SIX	V8 *	REAR AXLE
STANDARD	123-hp Six	162-hp V8	3.70 to 1 ratio
OVERDRIVE	123-hp Six	162-hp V8	4.11 to 1 ratio
AUTOMATIC	136-hp Six	162-hp V8	3.55 to 1 ratio

. . . And for performance that's really amazing, any of the above V8 power teams are available with Chevrolet's Super "Turbo-Fire" V8" that is rated at a full 180 horsepower.

THRIFTY "ONE-FIFTY" SERIES

All the new beauty of Motoramic Chevrolet lines and colors—enhanced with chrome on the hood ornament, front and rear emblems, radiator grille, bumpers and guards, all light rims, door handles, and hub caps—plus "Chevrolet" on the front fenders.

DISTINCTIVE "TWO-TEN" SERIES

Distinguished by additional chrome: in moldings around the windshield and rear window, on side window sills, and on the rear quarters in the forms of diagonal sash moldings that intersect horizontal rear fender moldings.

LUXURIOUS, BREATHTAKING BEL AIR SERIES

Highlighted by distinctive chrome around and between all window groups, the gold-plated Bel Air crest and chrome-plated name at the junctures of sash and extra-wide rear fender moldings, chrome "windsplit" moldings on front fenders, and chrome wheel disks.

BEL AIR 4-DOOR SEDAN . . . Model 2403

DISTINGUISHING FEATURES: Two of every five buyers select a 4-door sedan . . . and here is the leading 4-door of its field. Eighteen color selections (nine two-tones). All-steel body with large trunk. Crank-operated door windows and ventipanes; stationary rear quarter windows. Foam-rubber-cushioned seats for six. Two-tone pattern cloth, gabardine and vinyl upholstery color-keyed to exterior. Colored carpets. Three-spoke steering wheel, horn ring, windshield wipers and sun shades, lighted lockable glove compartment, electric clock, cigarette lighter, ash trays and built-in arm rests in front and rear, coat hooks, parcel shelf, and panel-controlled dome light with an automatic switch at each door.

CAR SIZE

Over-all length	195.6" (16.3 ft.)
Over-all width	74.0" (6.2 ft.)
Loaded height	60.5" (5.0 ft.)
Wheelbase	115.0" (9.6 ft.)
Wheel tread (av.)	58.4" (4.9 ft.)
Ramp angles	Front, 28°; rear, 16°

WEIGHT

(Add 130 lb. for gas and water; 150 for each passenger)

Power Team	6-Cyl. Engine	V8
Synchro-Mesh	3200 lb.	3170 lb.
Overdrive	3235 lb.	3205 lb.
Powerglide	3295 lb.	3265 lb.

HORSEPOWER

Power Team	6-Cyl. Engine	V8
Synchro-Mesh	123	162*
Overdrive	123	162*
Powerglide	136	162*

180 with 4-barrel carburetor and dual exhaust system.

ROOMINESS

	Rear	Front
Head room	35.4"	35.7"
Shoulder room	56.4"	56.8"
Hip room	63.0"	62.0"
Leg room	40.8"	43.1"
Total seat adjustment		4.4"

VISION AREA . . . . 24.4 sq. ft.

TRUNK CAPACITY . . . . 20.0 cu. ft.

"TWO-TEN" 4-DOOR SEDAN . . . Model 2103

DISTINGUISHING FEATURES: The favorite family car with six-passenger capacity. A choice of ten solid colors and eight two-tones. All-steel body with roomy trunk. Pattern cloth, gabardine, and vinyl upholstery, with all vinyl side walls—in two tones color-keyed to exterior. Colored rubber floor mats. Crank-operated door windows and venti- panes; stationary rear quarter windows. Foam-rubber-cushioned front seat, two-spoke steering wheel with horn ring, two windshield wipers and sun shades, lighted lockable glove compartment, cigarette lighter, ash trays and arm rests in front and rear, coat hooks, parcel shelf, and a panel-controlled dome light with automatic switches at both front doors.

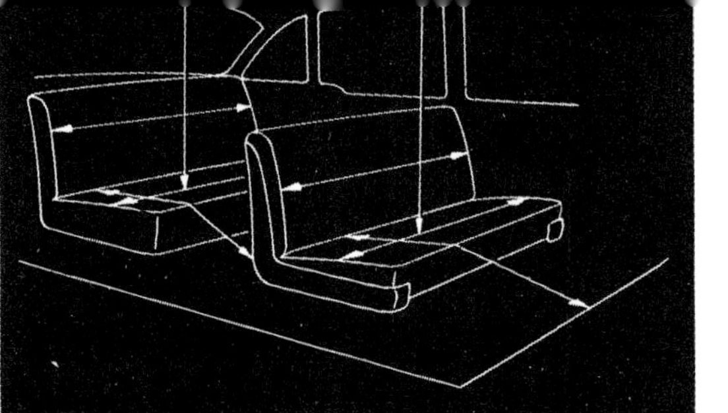

CAR SIZE

Over-all length	195.6″ (16.3 ft.)
Over-all width	74.0″ (6.2 ft.)
Loaded height	60.5″ (5.0 ft.)
Wheelbase	115.0″ (9.6 ft.)
Wheel tread (av.)	58.4″ (4.9 ft.)
Ramp angles	Front, 28°; rear, 16°

WEIGHT

(Add 130 lb. for gas and water; 150 for each passenger)

Power Team	6-Cyl. Engine	V8
Synchro-Mesh	3180 lb.	3150 lb.
Overdrive	3215 lb.	3185 lb.
Powerglide	3275 lb.	3245 lb.

HORSEPOWER

Power Team	6-Cyl. Engine	V8
Synchro-Mesh	123	162*
Overdrive	123	162*
Powerglide	136	162*

180 with 4-barrel carburetor and dual exhaust system.

ROOMINESS

	Rear	Front
Head room	35.4″	35.7″
Shoulder room	56.4″	56.8″
Hip room	63.0″	62.0″
Leg room	40.8″	43.1″
Total seat adjustment		4.4″

VISION AREA........24.4 sq. ft.

TRUNK CAPACITY........20.0 cu. ft.

"ONE-FIFTY" 4-DOOR SEDAN ... Model 1503

DISTINGUISHING FEATURES: An exceptional value for a full-size six-passenger car. A choice of ten solid colors and five two-tones. All-steel body with roomy trunk. Smart black and gray interior with pattern cloth and vinyl seat coverings, all-vinyl side walls, and black rubber floor mats. Crank-operated door windows and ventipanes, stationary rear quarter windows. High quality safety glass all around. Two-spoke steering wheel with horn button, two windshield wipers, a sun shade for the driver, lockable glove compartment, parcel shelf, and central dome light operated by the main light switch. Children can't open the rear doors of Chevrolets, while the sill buttons are down.

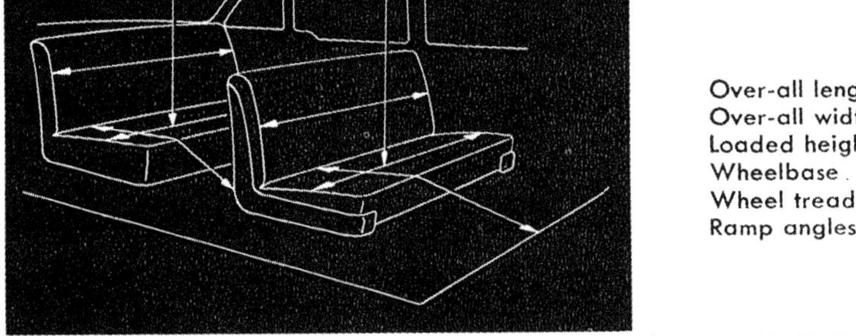

CAR SIZE

Over-all length	195.6" (16.3 ft.)
Over-all width	74.0" (6.2 ft.)
Loaded height	60.5" (5.0 ft.)
Wheelbase	115.0" (9.6 ft.)
Wheel tread (av.)	58.4" (4.9 ft.)
Ramp angles	Front, 28°; rear, 16°

WEIGHT

(Add 130 lb. for gas and water; 150 for each passenger)

Power Team	6-Cyl. Engine	V8
Synchro-Mesh	3165 lb.	3135 lb.
Overdrive	3200 lb.	3170 lb.
Powerglide	3260 lb.	3230 lb.

HORSEPOWER

Power Team	6-Cyl. Engine	V8
Synchro-Mesh	123	162*
Overdrive	123	162*
Powerglide	136	162*

180 with 4-barrel carburetor and dual exhaust system.

ROOMINESS

	Rear	Front
Head room	35.4"	35.7"
Shoulder room	56.4"	56.8"
Hip room	63.0"	62.0"
Leg room	40.8"	43.1"
Total seat adjustment		4.4"

VISION AREA. . . . . .24.4 sq. ft.

TRUNK CAPACITY. . . . . .20.0 cu. ft.

BEL AIR 2-DOOR SEDAN ... Model 2402

DISTINGUISHING FEATURES: Three of every ten buyers favor 2-door sedans because of their smart appearance and convenience features. A choice of nine solid colors and nine two-tones. All-steel six-passenger body with spacious trunk. Foam-rubber-cushioned seats; center-fold front-seat back rests. Deep pile carpets. Crank-operated ventipanes and side windows. Pattern cloth, gabardine, and vinyl interior—in two tones color-keyed to exterior. Three-spoke steering wheel with horn ring, two windshield wipers and sun shades, lighted lockable glove compartment, electric clock, cigarette lighter, ash trays and arm rests in front and rear (built-in type in front), assist straps, coat hooks, parcel shelf, and a panel-controlled dome light with automatic switches at both doors.

CAR SIZE

Over-all length	195.6" (16.3 ft.)
Over-all width	74.0" (6.2 ft.)
Loaded height	60.5" (5.0 ft.)
Wheelbase	115.0" (9.6 ft.)
Wheel tread (av.)	58.4" (4.9 ft.)
Ramp angles	Front, 28°; rear, 16°

WEIGHT

(Add 130 lb. for gas and water; 150 for each passenger)

Power Team	6-Cyl. Engine	V8
Synchro-Mesh	3155 lb.	3125 lb.
Overdrive	3190 lb.	3160 lb.
Powerglide	3250 lb.	3220 lb.

HORSEPOWER

Power Team	6-Cyl. Engine	V8
Synchro-Mesh	123	162*
Overdrive	123	162*
Powerglide	136	162*

180 with 4-barrel carburetor and dual exhaust system.

ROOMINESS

	Rear	Front
Head room	35.4"	35.7"
Shoulder room	56.6"	56.6"
Hip room	62.9"	61.8"
Leg room	40.8"	43.1"
Total seat adjustment		4.4"

VISION AREA............24.7 sq. ft.

TRUNK CAPACITY..........20.0 cu. ft.

"TWO-TEN" 2-DOOR SEDAN . . . Model 2102

DISTINGUISHING FEATURES: Parents with small children often prefer a 2-door sedan. This one is available in eight two-tones and ten solid colors. All steel body with extra-large doors and roomy trunk. Front seat is foam-rubber-cushioned and has center-fold back rests. Pattern cloth, gabardine and vinyl interior—with all-vinyl side walls and rubber floor mats—in two tones, color-keyed to exterior. Crank-operated ventipanes and windows. Two-spoke steering wheel, horn ring, two windshield wipers and sun shades, lighted lockable glove compartment, cigarette lighter, ash trays, arm rests, assist straps, coat hooks, parcel shelf, and a panel-controlled dome light, automatic switches at both doors.

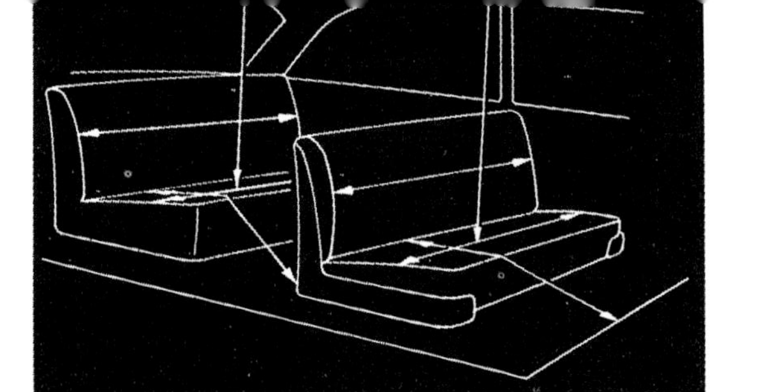

CAR SIZE

Over-all length	195.6" (16.3 ft.)
Over-all width	74.0" (6.2 ft.)
Loaded height	60.5" (5.0 ft.)
Wheelbase	115.0" (9.6 ft.)
Wheel tread (av.)	58.4" (4.9 ft.)
Ramp angles	Front, 28°; rear, 16°

WEIGHT

(Add 130 lb. for gas and water; 150 for each passenger)

Power Team	6-Cyl. Engine	V8
Synchro-Mesh	3145 lb.	3115 lb.
Overdrive	3180 lb.	3150 lb.
Powerglide	3240 lb.	3210 lb.

HORSEPOWER

Power Team	6-Cyl. Engine	V8
Synchro-Mesh	123	162*
Overdrive	123	162*
Powerglide	136	162*

180 with 4-barrel carburetor and dual exhaust system.

ROOMINESS

	Rear	Front
Head room	35.4"	35.7"
Shoulder room	56.6"	56.6"
Hip room	62.9"	61.8"
Leg room	40.8"	43.1"
Total seat adjustment		4.4"

VISION AREA . . . . .24.7 sq. ft.

TRUNK CAPACITY . . . . .20.0 cu. ft.

"TWO-TEN" DELRAY CLUB COUPE ... Model 2124

DISTINGUISHING FEATURES: A full-size six-passenger model with ultra-smart interior. Available in six solid colors and seven two-tones (three exclusive). All-steel body with extra-large doors and spacious trunk. Crank-operated ventipanes and side windows. Foam-rubber-cushioned front seat with center-fold back rests. Special two-color all-vinyl interior, color-keyed to exterior. Colored carpets, two-spoke steering wheel with horn ring, two windshield wipers and sun shades, lighted lockable glove compartment, cigarette lighter, ash trays and arm rests in front and rear, assist straps, coat hooks, parcel shelf, and a dome light operated by the light switch or automatic door switches.

CAR SIZE

Over-all length	195.6" (16.3 ft.)
Over-all width	74.0" (6.2 ft.)
Loaded height	60.5" (5.0 ft.)
Wheelbase	115.0" (9.6 ft.)
Wheel tread (av.)	58.4" (4.9 ft.)
Ramp angles	Front, 28°; rear, 16°

WEIGHT

(Add 130 lb. for gas and water; 150 for each passenger)

Power Team	6-Cyl. Engine	V8
Synchro-Mesh	3145 lb.	3115 lb.
Overdrive	3180 lb.	3150 lb.
Powerglide	3240 lb.	3210 lb.

HORSEPOWER

Power Team	6-Cyl. Engine	V8
Synchro-Mesh	123	162*
Overdrive	123	162*
Powerglide	136	162*

*180 with 4-barrel carburetor and dual exhaust system.

ROOMINESS

	Rear	Front
Head room	35.4"	35.7"
Shoulder room	56.6"	56.6"
Hip room	62.9"	61.8"
Leg room	40.8"	43.1"
Total seat adjustment		4.4"

VISION AREA ....24.7 sq. ft.

TRUNK CAPACITY ....20.0 cu. ft.

"ONE-FIFTY" 2-DOOR SEDAN . . . Model 1502

DISTINGUISHING FEATURES: A smart, practical six-passenger model—at lowest cost—in a choice of ten solid colors and five two-tones. All-steel body with extra-large doors and spacious trunk. Center-fold front-seat back rests. Crank-operated ventipanes and side windows. High quality safety glass all around, as in all Chevrolets. Gray and black interior in pattern cloth and vinyl, with all-vinyl side walls, and black rubber floor mats. Two-spoke steering wheel with horn button, two windshield wipers, a sun shade for the driver, lockable glove compartment, parcel shelf, and panel-controlled central dome light.

CAR SIZE

Over-all length	195.6" (16.3 ft.)
Over-all width	74.0" (6.2 ft.)
Loaded height	60.5" (5.0 ft.)
Wheelbase	115.0" (9.6 ft.)
Wheel tread (av.)	58.4" (4.9 ft.)
Ramp angles	Front, 28°; rear, 16°

WEIGHT

(Add 130 lb. for gas and water; 150 for each passenger)

Power Team	6-Cyl. Engine	V8
Synchro-Mesh	3110 lb.	3080 lb.
Overdrive	3145 lb.	3115 lb.
Powerglide	3205 lb.	3175 lb.

HORSEPOWER

Power Team	6-Cyl. Engine	V8
Synchro-Mesh	123	162*
Overdrive	123	162*
Powerglide	136	162*

180 with 4-barrel carburetor and dual exhaust system.

ROOMINESS

	Rear	Front
Head room	35.4"	35.7"
Shoulder room	56.6"	56.6"
Hip room	62.9"	61.8"
Leg room	40.8"	43.1"
Total seat adjustment		4.4"

VISION AREA . . . . .24.7 sq. ft.

TRUNK CAPACITY . . . . .20.0 cu. ft.

"ONE-FIFTY" UTILITY SEDAN ... Model 1512

DISTINGUISHING FEATURES: With 51 cubic feet of stowage space, this model is a practical car for the businessman who needs extra carrying capacity. A choice of ten solid colors and five two-tones. All-steel body with two extra-large doors, roomy trunk, and load compartment behind the three-passenger driver's seat. Center-fold seat back rests. Gray and black interior with pattern cloth and vinyl seat upholstery, vinyl door panels, composition-board load-compartment walls, and black rubber floor mats. Crank-operated ventipanes and door windows; stationary rear quarter windows. Two-spoke steering wheel with horn button, two windshield wipers, a sun shade for the driver, lockable glove compartment, parcel shelf, and a panel-controlled dome light.

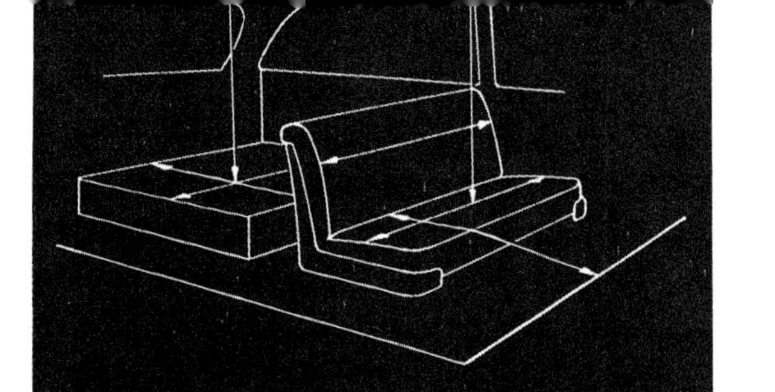

CAR SIZE

Over-all length	195.6" (16.3 ft.)
Over-all width	74.0" (6.2 ft.)
Loaded height	60.5" (5.0 ft.)
Wheelbase	115.0" (9.6 ft.)
Wheel tread (av.)	58.4" (4.9 ft.)
Ramp angles	Front, 28°; rear, 16°

WEIGHT

(Add 130 lb. for gas and water; 150 for each passenger)

Power Team	6-Cyl. Engine	V8
Synchro-Mesh	3085 lb.	3055 lb.
Overdrive	3120 lb.	3090 lb.
Powerglide	3180 lb.	3150 lb.

HORSEPOWER

Power Team	6-Cyl. Engine	V8
Synchro-Mesh	123	162*
Overdrive	123	162*
Powerglide	136	162*

180 with 4-barrel carburetor and dual exhaust system.

FRONT SEAT ROOM

Head room	35.7"	Shoulder room	56.6"
Leg room	43.1"	Hip room	61.8"
	Total adjustment	4.4"	

LOAD COMPARTMENT

Height	43.7" to top, 23.0" to window
Length and width at floor	36.4" x 61.0"
Capacity	31 cu. ft. (trunk 20 cu. ft.)

VISION AREA .... 24.6 sq. ft.

BEL AIR SPORT COUPE ... Model 2454

DISTINGUISHING FEATURES: A style pace setter—admired by all. Choice of five solid colors, and eight two-tones with regular or special color treatment. All-steel hardtop body with extra-large doors, roomy trunk. Crank-operated ventipanes and windows. Foam-rubber-cushioned seats; center-fold front-seat backs. Straw-pattern cloth and vinyl upholstery; all-vinyl side walls and head-lining—in two tones color-keyed to exterior. Colored carpets. Chrome roof bows, rails, and rear window frame. Three-spoke steering wheel with horn ring, two windshield wipers and sun shades, lighted lockable glove compartment, electric clock, cigarette lighter, ash trays, built-in arm rests, parcel shelf, and two panel-controlled corner lights with automatic door switches.

CAR SIZE

Over-all length	195.6" (16.3 ft.)
Over-all width	74.0" (6.2 ft.)
Loaded height	59.1" (4.9 ft.)
Wheelbase	115.0" (9.6 ft.)
Wheel tread (av.)	58.4" (4.9 ft.)
Ramp angles	Front, 28°; rear, 16°

WEIGHT

(Add 130 lb. for gas and water; 150 for each passenger)

Power Team	6-Cyl. Engine	V8
Synchro-Mesh	3195 lb.	3165 lb.
Overdrive	3230 lb.	3200 lb.
Powerglide	3290 lb.	3260 lb.

HORSEPOWER

Power Team	6-Cyl. Engine	V8
Synchro-Mesh	123	162*
Overdrive	123	162*
Powerglide	136	162*

*180 with 4-barrel carburetor and dual exhaust system.

ROOMINESS

	Rear	Front
Head room	34.0"	34.8"
Shoulder room	56.7"	56.8"
Hip room	54.2"	61.8"
Leg room	37.3"	43.0"
Total seat adjustment		4.4"

VISION AREA.............23.1 sq. ft.

TRUNK CAPACITY..........20.0 cu. ft.

BEL AIR CONVERTIBLE . . . Model 2434

DISTINGUISHING FEATURES: Designed for the youthful, in age or spirit. A choice of three solid colors and seven special two-tones, with color-keyed top. Specially reinforced body with roomy trunk. Hydraulically operated top with zippered-in plastic rear window. Foam-rubber-cushioned seats; center-fold front-seat back rests. Crank-operated ventipanes; side windows that lower flush with chrome sills. All-vinyl interior, with matching top boot, color-keyed to exterior. Colored carpets. Chrome windshield inside molding. Three-spoke steering wheel with horn ring, two windshield wipers and sun shades, lighted lockable glove compartment, electric clock, cigarette lighter, ash trays, built-in arm rests, and two panel-controlled courtesy lights with automatic door switches.

CAR SIZE

Over-all length	195.6" (16.3 ft.)
Over-all width	74.0" (6.2 ft.)
Loaded height (top up)	59.1" (4.9 ft.)
Wheelbase	115.0" (9.6 ft.)
Wheel tread (av.)	58.4" (4.9 ft.)
Ramp angles	Front, 28°; rear, 16°

WEIGHT

(Add 130 lb. for gas and water; 150 for each passenger)

Power Team	6-Cyl. Engine	V8
Synchro-Mesh	3315 lb.	3285 lb.
Overdrive	3350 lb.	3320 lb.
Powerglide	3410 lb.	3380 lb.

HORSEPOWER

Power Team	6-Cyl. Engine	V8
Synchro-Mesh	123	162*
Overdrive	123	162*
Powerglide	136	162*

180 with 4-barrel carburetor and dual exhaust system.

ROOMINESS

	Rear	Front
Head room	34.0"	34.6"
Shoulder room	48.4"	56.8"
Hip room	50.1"	61.8"
Leg room	37.5"	43.0"
Total seat adjustment		4.4"

VISION AREA ....19.7 sq. ft.

TRUNK CAPACITY ....17.0 cu. ft.

BEL AIR BEAUVILLE ... Model 2409

DISTINGUISHING FEATURES: The finest of station wagons—in a choice of four solid colors and four two-tones. All-steel body with large load compartment, four doors, end gates. Two full-width seats (front seat foam-rubber-cushioned); folding rear seat forms extension of linoleum-surfaced load platform. Crank-operated ventipanes and door windows; wraparound rear quarter windows. All-vinyl interior (with straw-pattern cloth on portions of seats) in two tones color-keyed to exterior. Colored rubber floor mats. Three-spoke steering wheel, horn ring, two windshield wipers and sun shades, lighted lockable glove compartment, electric clock, cigarette lighter, ash trays, built-in front arm rests, coat hooks and a panel-controlled dome light with an automatic switch at each door.

CAR SIZE

Over-all length	197.1" (16.4 ft.)
Over-all width	74.0" (6.2 ft.)
Loaded height	60.8" (5.1 ft.)
Wheelbase	115.0" (9.6 ft.)
Wheel tread (av.)	58.4" (4.9 ft.)
Ramp angles	Front, 28°; rear, 16°

WEIGHT

(Add 130 lb. for gas and water; 150 for each passenger)

Power Team	6-Cyl. Engine	V8
Synchro-Mesh	3385 lb.	3355 lb.
Overdrive	3420 lb.	3390 lb.
Powerglide	3480 lb.	3450 lb.

HORSEPOWER

Power Team	6-Cyl. Engine	V8
Synchro-Mesh	123	162*
Overdrive	123	162*
Powerglide	136	162*

180 with 4-barrel carburetor and dual exhaust system.

SITTING ROOM

	Rear	Front
Head room	35.4"	35.8"
Shoulder room	56.5"	56.8"
Hip room	62.3"	61.9"
Leg room	43.1"	43.3"
Total seat adjustment		4.4"

LOAD COMPARTMENT . . See pages 40-41

VISION AREA . . . . .27.6 sq. ft.

"TWO-TEN" TOWNSMAN   . . . Model 2109

DISTINGUISHING FEATURES: Ideal transportation for modern suburban living—four solid colors and four two-tones. All-steel body with large load compartment, end gates, four doors. Two full-width seats (front seat foam-rubber-cushioned); rear seat folds level with linoleum-covered load platform. Crank-operated ventipanes and door windows; wrap-around rear quarter windows. Two-tone all-vinyl interior, rubber floor mats—color-keyed to exterior. Two-spoke steering wheel, horn ring, two windshield wipers and sun shades, lighted lockable glove compartment, cigarette lighter, ash trays, front arm rests, coat hooks, panel-controlled dome light with automatic switches at front doors.

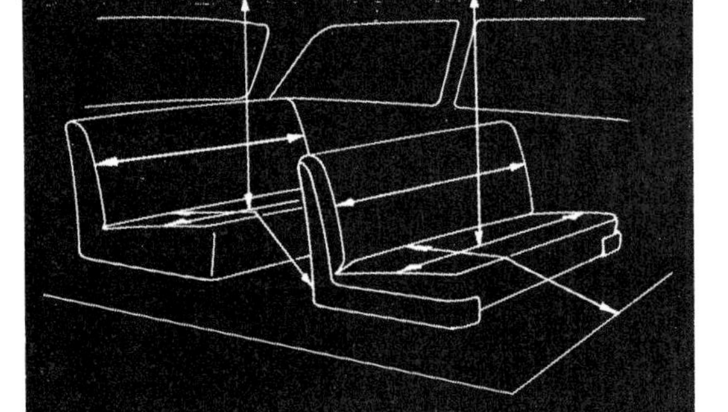

CAR SIZE

Over-all length	197.1" (16.4 ft.)
Over-all width	74.0" (6.2 ft.)
Loaded height	60.8" (5.1 ft.)
Wheelbase	115.0" (9.6 ft.)
Wheel tread (av.)	58.4" (4.9 ft.)
Ramp angles	Front, 28°; rear, 16°

WEIGHT

(Add 130 lb. for gas and water; 150 for each passenger)

Power Team	6-Cyl. Engine	V8
Synchro-Mesh	3370 lb.	3340 lb.
Overdrive	3405 lb.	3375 lb.
Powerglide	3465 lb.	3435 lb.

HORSEPOWER

Power Team	6-Cyl. Engine	V8
Synchro-Mesh	123	162*
Overdrive	123	162*
Powerglide	136	162*

180 with 4-barrel carburetor and dual exhaust system.

SITTING ROOM

	Rear	Front
Head room	35.4"	35.8"
Shoulder room	56.5"	56.8"
Hip room	62.3"	61.9"
Leg room	43.1"	43.3"
Total seat adjustment		4.4"

LOAD COMPARTMENT ..See pages 40-41

VISION AREA ....27.6 sq. ft.

"TWO-TEN" HANDYMAN ... Model 2129

DISTINGUISHING FEATURES: Dedicated to the modern trend to live differently and better. Eight color selections, four of them two-tones. All-steel body with large load compartment, end gates, two extra-large doors. Two full-width seats. Front seat is foam-rubber cushioned and has center-fold back rests; folding rear seat forms forward extension of linoleum-covered load platform.

Crank-operated ventipanes, door windows, and center windows; wraparound rear quarter windows. All-vinyl interior with rubber floor mats—in two tones color-keyed to exterior. Two-spoke steering wheel with horn ring, two windshield wipers and sun shades, lighted lockable glove compartment, cigarette lighter, ash trays, front seat arm rests, panel-controlled dome light with automatic door switches

CAR SIZE

Over-all length	197.1"	(16.4 ft.)
Over-all width	74.0"	(6.2 ft.)
Loaded height	60.8"	(5.1 ft.)
Wheelbase	115.0"	(9.6 ft.)
Wheel tread (av.)	58.4"	(4.9 ft.)
Ramp angles		Front, 28°; rear, 16°

WEIGHT

(Add 130 lb. for gas and water; 150 for each passenger)

Power Team	6-Cyl. Engine	V8
Synchro-Mesh	3330 lb.	3300 lb.
Overdrive	3365 lb.	3335 lb.
Powerglide	3425 lb.	3395 lb.

HORSEPOWER

Power Team	6-Cyl. Engine	V8
Synchro-Mesh	123	162*
Overdrive	123	162*
Powerglide	136	162*

*180 with 4-barrel carburetor and dual exhaust system.

SITTING ROOM

	Rear	Front
Head room	35.4"	35.8"
Shoulder room	56.5"	56.9"
Hip room	61.7"	61.8"
Leg room	43.1"	43.3"
Total seat adjustment		4.4"

LOAD COMPARTMENT . . See pages 40-41

VISION AREA . . . .**28.1 sq. ft.**

"ONE-FIFTY" HANDYMAN . . . Model 1529

DISTINGUISHING FEATURES: The thriftiest of handymen in a choice of three solid colors and two two-tones. All-steel body with large load compartment, two extra-large doors, and end gates. Two full-width seats, seating six; center-fold front-seat back rests; folding rear seat forms forward extension of linoleum-surfaced load platform. Crank-operated ventipanes and door windows, stationary center windows and wrap-around rear quarter windows. Two-tone all-vinyl interior, color-keyed to exterior. Black rubber floor mats. Two-spoke steering wheel with horn button, a sun shade for the driver, lockable glove compartment, and dome light operated by instrument panel light switch.

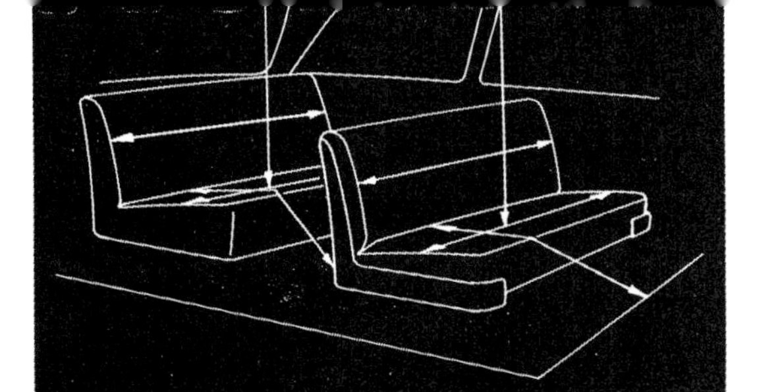

SITTING ROOM

	Rear	Front
Head room	35.4"	35.8"
Shoulder room	56.5"	56.9"
Hip room	61.7"	61.8"
Leg room	43.1"	43.3"
Total seat adjustment		4.4"

LOAD COMPARTMENT . . See pages 40-41

VISION AREA . . . . **27-9 sq. ft.**

CAR SIZE

Over-all length	197.1" (16.4 ft.)
Over-all width	74.0" (6.2 ft.)
Loaded height	60.8" (5.1 ft.)
Wheelbase	115.0" (9.6 ft.)
Wheel tread (av.)	58.4" (4.9 ft.)
Ramp angles	Front, 28°; rear, 16°

WEIGHT

(Add 130 lb. for gas and water; 150 for each passenger)

Power Team	6-Cyl. Engine	V8
Synchro-Mesh	3290 lb.	3260 lb.
Overdrive	3325 lb.	3295 lb.
Powerglide	3385 lb.	3355 lb.

HORSEPOWER

Power Team	6-Cyl. Engine	V8
Synchro-Mesh	123	162*
Overdrive	123	162*
Powerglide	136	162*

*180 with 4-barrel carburetor and dual exhaust system.

THE HIGHLY USABLE

STATION WAGON LOAD COMPARTMENT

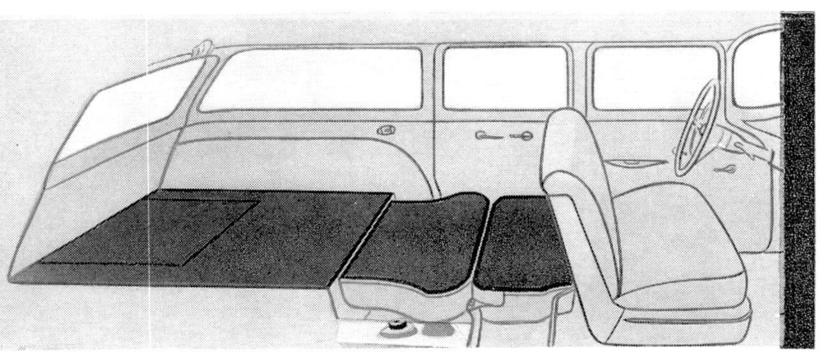

AMPLE DIMENSIONS • • •	Seat Up	Seat Down
Platform length to tail gate	47.0"	84.4"
Platform length to end of tail gate	68.7"	106.1"
Maximum load space width	58.3"	58.3"
Width between wheelhouses	46.1"	46.1"
Height—from platform to top	36.9"	36.9"
Capacity—from platform to window sill (cu. ft.)	45.0	87.0

LARGE REAR OPENING • • •	
Width	43.6"
Height	28.3"
Approximate tail gate loading height with vehicle empty	30.0"

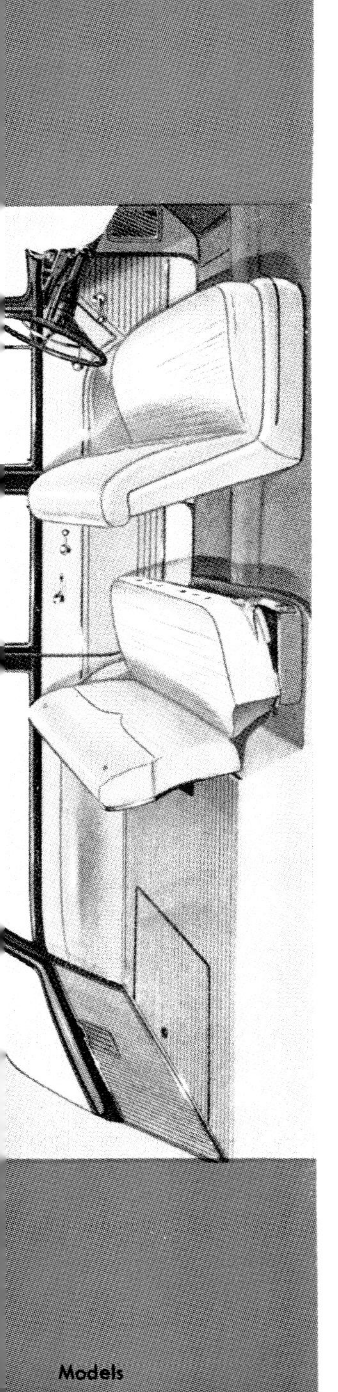

• • • **AND IMPORTANT FEATURES:** The large steel platform is lengthened to more than seven feet by folding the rear seat and is extended further, by lowering the tailgate, to provide a load support of nearly nine feet. Durable ribbed linoleum covers this entire surface. The spare wheel, in its well below the platform, is reached by lifting out a section of the platform. The rear side doors of 4-door models give direct access to the load space; in 2-door models, curbside loading is made possible by the center-folding front-seat back rests. The double-walled tail-

gate is supported by two sturdy hinges and stout steel cables that retract as the gate is closed. The gate's central handle turns to release slam latches in the sides of the gate. The regular car key operates the weather-protected lock in the handle. A dovetail on the gate's top engages a wedge to lock the lift gate. The box-sectioned lift gate, framing the rear window, lifts to two positions on concealed hinges and is held up by self-latching telescoping supports. To close the gate, releases at the supports are disengaged and the gate is lifted slightly before lowering.

EXTERIOR COLOR COMBINATIONS

14 Dramatic Solid Exteriors
and
21 Striking Two-Tones
in Two Styles

. . . with harmonious
two-tone interiors

	4-DOOR SEDANS			2-DOOR SEDAN TYPES					BEL AIR SPORT TYPES			STATION WAGONS 4-DOOR		STATION WAGONS 2-DOOR	
	Bel Air	"Two-Ten"	"One-Fifty"	Bel Air Sedan	"Two-Ten" Sedan	"Two-Ten" Club Coupe	"One-Fifty" Sedan	"One-Fifty" Utility Sedan	Sport Coupe	Sport Coupe (Spec. 2-tones)	Convertible	Bel Air	"Two-Ten"	"Two-Ten"	"One-Fifty"
Neptune GREEN—a cool dark green	A	A	Z	A	A	D	Z	Z	E			O	A	A	A
Sea-Mist GREEN—a soft pale green	A	A	Z	A	A	D	Z	Z							A
Neptune GREEN below Sea-Mist GREEN	A	A	Z	A	A		Z	Z					A	A	A
Sea-Mist GREEN below Neptune GREEN											B	O			
Neptune GREEN below Shoreline BEIGE	A	A	Z	A	A		Z	Z	E	E					
Shoreline BEIGE below Neptune GREEN									E	E					
Sea-Mist GREEN below India IVORY		A			A	D									
Harvest GOLD—the gold of ripe grain									E						
Harvest GOLD below India IVORY	A			A		D			E	E	C				
Glacier BLUE—chill, clean dark blue	F	F	Z	F	F	H	Z	Z	I			I	H	H	
Skyline BLUE—a light sky blue	F	F	Z	F	F	H	Z	Z	I						
Glacier BLUE below Skyline BLUE	F	F	Z	F	F		Z	Z							
Skyline BLUE below Glacier BLUE											G		H	H	
Glacier BLUE below Shoreline BEIGE									I	I		I	H	H	
Shoreline BEIGE below Glacier BLUE		F			F	H									
Skyline BLUE below India IVORY	F	F	Z	F	F	H	Z	Z	I	I					

Shadow GRAY—a quiet dignified gray	F	F	Z	F	F		Z	Z						
Shadow GRAY below India IVORY	F	F	Z	F	F		Z	Z						
Onyx BLACK—smart popular black	F	F	Z	F	F	Y	Z	Z	S	P				
India IVORY—a pale off-white tone	F	F	Z	F	F	Y	Z	Z						
Onyx BLACK below India IVORY						Y								
India IVORY below Onyx BLACK						Y								
Gypsy RED—a fiery and dashing red										R				
Gypsy RED below India IVORY						Y								
Gypsy RED below Shoreline BEIGE									S S	R	O			
Autumn BRONZE—a rich dark brown		K	Z		K		Z	Z				L	L	N
Shoreline BEIGE—a light sandy tone	L	K	Z	L	K		Z	Z	S		I	L	L	
Autumn BRONZE below Shoreline BEIGE	L	K		L	K					M	O			N
Shoreline BEIGE below Autumn BRONZE												L	L	
Copper MAROON—a dark metallic color	L	K	Z	L	K		Z	Z						
CORAL—the pale pink of coral										U				
CORAL below India IVORY										U				
CORAL below Shadow GRAY	T			T					T T					
Regal TURQUOISE—a bright green-blue											O			
Regal TURQUOISE below India IVORY	V			V					X X	W				
190 COLOR-MODEL COMBINATIONS	18	18	15	18	18	13	15	15	21	10	8	8	8	5

INTERIOR COLORS: A Two-tone GREEN. B Two-tone GREEN with GREEN top. C Two-tone GREEN with WHITE top. D GREEN and BEIGE. E GREEN and STRAW • F Two-tone BLUE. G Two-tone BLUE with BLUE top. H BLUE and BEIGE. I BLUE and STRAW • K Two-tone BROWN. L BEIGE and BROWN. M BEIGE and BROWN with BEIGE top. N STRAW and BROWN • O BEIGE and STRAW. P BEIGE and RED with WHITE top. R BEIGE and RED with BEIGE top. S RED and STRAW • T CORAL and GRAY. U CORAL and GRAY with WHITE top • V IVORY and TURQUOISE. W IVORY and TURQUOISE with WHITE top. X TURQUOISE and STRAW • Y BLACK and IVORY. Z GRAY and BLACK.

WELL-EQUIPPED STANDARD MODELS

A comparison of the appointments and trim that distinguish the different models. In some instances, appointments that are standard in some models are available at extra cost (E) in other models.

	4-DOOR SEDANS			2-DOOR SEDAN TYPES					SPORT TYPES		STATION WAGONS 4-DOOR		2-DOOR	
	Bel Air	"Two-Ten"	"One-Fifty"	Bel Air Sedan	"Two-Ten" Sedan	"Two-Ten" Club Coupe	"One-Fifty" Sedan	"One-Fifty" Utility	Bel Air Sport Coupe	Bel Air Convertible	Bel Air	"Two-Ten"	"Two-Ten"	"One-Fifty"
Arm rests, Front	•	•	E	•	•	•	E	E	•	•	•	•	•	E
Arm rests, Rear	•	•	E	•	•	•	E		•	•				
Ash tray, Instrument panel	•	•	E	•	•	•	E	E	•	•	•	•	•	E
Ash tray, Rear	•	•		2	2	2			2	2				
Assist straps				•	•	•								
Carpets (Rubber floor mats for others)	•			•		•			•	•				
Chrome moldings, Exterior:														
Fender moldings, Front	•			•					•	•	•			
Fender moldings, Rear	•	•		•	•	•			•	•	•	•	•	
Light frames	•	•	•	•	•	•	•	•	•	•	•	•	•	•
Rear window moldings	•	•		•	•	•			•		•	•	•	
Side sash or wing moldings	Sash	Sash		Sash	Sash	Sash			Sash	Sash	Wing	Wing	Wing	
Side window loop or sill moldings	Loop	Sill		Loop	Sill	Sill			Loop	Sill				
Side window saddle moldings									•	•				
Side window sill and top moldings											•	•	•	
Windshield pillar moldings	•			•					•	•	•			
Windshield reveal molding	•	•		•	•	•			•	•	•	•	•	

Chrome moldings, Interior:														
Instrument panel center molding	•			•					•	•	•			
Roof bows, rails; rear window molding									•					
Scuff pad moldings, seat and side wall	•	*		•	*	*			•	•	•	•	*	*
Windshield garnish molding										•				
Cigarette lighter	•	•	E	•	•	•	E	E	•	•	•	•	•	E
Clock, Electric	•	E	E	•	E	E	E	E	•	•	•	E	E	E
Coat hooks	•	•		•	•	•			•	•	•	•		
Glove compartment automatic light	•	•	E	•	•	•	E	E	•	•	•	•	•	E
Glove compartment key lock	•	•	•	•	•	•	•	•	•	•	•	•	•	•
Horn ring, Full-circle (Button for others)	•	•		•	•	•			•	•	•	•	•	
Light automatic door switches, Inside	4	2		2	2	2			2	2	4	2	2	
Lights, Inside	1	1	1	1	1	1	1	1	2	2	1	1	1	1
Locks, Car key (On both front doors)	•	•	•	•	•	•	•	•	•	•	•	•	•	•
Package shelf	•	•	•	•	•	•	•	•	•		•			
Rear view mirror, Inside	•	•	•	•	•	•	•	•	•	•	•	•	•	
Roof panel sound insulation, Extra	•	•		•	•	•			•	•	•	•	•	
Seat cushion pad, Foam rubber front	•	•		•	•	•			•	•	•	•	•	
Seat cushion pad, Foam rubber rear	•			•					•	•	•	•		
Steering wheel, 3-spoke (Others 2-spoke)	•			•					•		•			
Sun shade, Left side	•	•	•	•	•	•	•	•	•	•	•	•	•	•
Sun shade, Right side	•	•	E	•	•	•	E	E	•	•	•	•	•	E
Ventipane crank regulators, Front	•	•	•	•	•	•	•	•	•	•	•	•	•	•
Wheel disks, Full-size (Others hub caps)	•	E	E	•	E	E	E	E	•	•	•	E	E	E
Windshield wipers, Dual vacuum-operated	•	•	•	•	•	•	•	•	•	•	•	•	•	•

*Seat only.

A WONDERFUL SELECTION
OF OPTIONAL AND ACCESSORY EQUIPMENT

Factory-installed options and dealer-installed accessories, available at extra cost on every Motoramic Chevrolet (except as noted):

Accelerator pedal cover, Rubber....................Accessory

Air cleaner, One-pint oil bath...............Option on 6-cylinder models

Air conditioner................Option for all V8 models but Convertible

Arm rests, Front and rear............Accessory for "One-Fifty" models

Ash tray, Instrument panel...........Accessory for "One-Fifty" models

Back-up lights....................Accessory

Body sill moldings, Chrome....................Accessory

Brake signal light, Parking....................Accessory

Brakes, Vacuum-power....................Option

Cigarette lighter................Accessory for "One-Fifty" models

Clock, Electric.........Accessory for "Two-Ten" and "One-Fifty" models

Clutch, Heavy-duty....................Option

Color combinations, Two-tone exterior....................Option

Compass, Illuminated....................Accessory

Convertible top lift, Moisture-sensitive..........Accessory for Convertible

Courtesy lights....................Accessory for all but Convertible

Direction signals, Self-cancelling.............Factory-installed accessory

Door edge guards, Chrome..........Accessory for all but station wagons

Door handle shields, Chrome....................Accessory

Dual exhaust and 4-barrel carburetor............Option for V8 models

Engine compartment automatic light....................Accessory

Engine ventilation system, Positive....................Option

Fender guards, Chrome (on ends of bumpers)............Accessory

Fender shields, Chrome (on sides of front fenders)..........Accessory

Floor mats, Colored rubber....................Accessory

Gasoline tank filler cap, Locking....................Accessory

Gasoline tank filler door guard, Chrome....................Accessory

Generator, 30-ampere....................Option

Generator, 40-ampere low cut-in....................Option

Glass, E-Z-Eye tinted safety plate (with or without shaded
    windshield band)....................Option

Glove compartment automatic light.....Accessory for "One-Fifty" models

Governor....................Option for models with 123-hp engine

Heater and defroster, Air-flow .... Factory-installed Accessory
Heater and defroster, Recirculating .... Factory-installed Accessory
License plate frame, Chrome.................................Accessory
Mirror, Vanity sun shade.....................................Accessory
Mirrors, Rear view.................................See rear view mirrors
Oil filter, One-quart..Option
Radiator grille guard, Chrome.................................Accessory
Radio Antenna..Accessory
Radio, Manual tuning...Accessory
Radio, Push-button...Accessory
Radio, Signal-seeking..Accessory
Radio speaker, Auxiliary (rear seat)
...................Accessory for all but Convertible and station wagons
Rain deflectors, Chrome side window .... Accessory for sedan types
Rear view mirror, Inside non-glare.............................Accessory
Rear view mirror, Outside body-mount..........................Accessory
Rear view mirror, Outside remote control.......................Accessory
Seat adjustment control,
    Electric-power.............Option for Bel Air and "Two-Ten" models
Seat covers, Fiber..Accessory
Seat covers, Nylon...Accessory
Seat covers, Plastic..Accessory
Seat cushion covers, Nylon....................................Accessory
Shaver, Electric..Accessory
Spot light, Portable..Accessory

Spot light, Remote control left side (with rear view mirror)......Accessory
Springs, Chassis heavy-duty rear................................Option
Steering, Hydraulic-power......................................Option
Sun shade, Right side.................Accessory for "One-Fifty" models
Sun Visor, Windshield Outside........Accessory for all but Convertible
Tires, Six-ply 6.70-15...Option
Tires, Whitewall 4- or 6-ply 6.70-15...........................Option
Tissue dispenser, Chrome....................................Accessory
Tool kit with bag...Accessory
Traffic light viewer...Accessory
Transmission, Overdrive..Option
Transmission, Powerglide.......................................Option
Trunk automatic light..............Accessory for all but station wagons
Wheel carrier, Continental-type
    outside.......................Accessory for all but station wagons
Wheel disks, Full-size
    chrome.............Accessory for "Two-Ten" and "One-Fifty" models
Wheel moldings,
    Chrome.............Accessory for "Two-Ten" and "One-Fifty" models
Window controls, Electric-power.Option for Bel Air and "Two-Ten" models
Windshield glare shield.....................................Accessory
Windshield washer, Foot-operated.............................Accessory
Windshield washer, Vacuum-operated..........................Accessory
Windshield washer and wiper action co-ordinator, Automatic.....Accessory
Windshield wiper blades.....................................Accessory
Windshield wipers, Dual electric...............................Option

CHEVROLET . . . A CAR OF HIGHEST QUALITY AT LOWEST COST

With 14 beautiful models in 190 model-color selections, the Motoramic Chevrolet provides every practical combination of features that is available in any car—and at less cost.

Chevrolet's policy is that of providing all the features that assure the best values in every Chevrolet. The body styles in each series are those that are most wanted by most people. The color selections for each body style are those that make it look its best. And the options and accessories for each model are those that provide the best performance, the greatest comfort, convenience, and service, and the best appearance in that particular model.

Chevrolet quality exceeds that of other low-cost cars and equals that of cars that cost much more. Not only is this quality designed into the car itself but into all options and all accessories. In fact, every option and every accessory is developed as an integral part of the car with the same high standards as other Chevrolet parts.

With Chevrolet's wide variety of selections, there is a model to fit everyone's needs. For whatever body style the customer may want, whatever styling, color, trim, or conveniences he may desire, whatever kind of performance he may prefer—the Motoramic Chevrolet will provide just the combination to suit his needs, his taste, and his budget.

Sized for Comfort and Maneuverability

- Plenty of passenger and luggage room—for comfort.
- Long wheelbase in relation to overall length—for riding ease.
- Steep ramp angles—for going up and down sharp grades.
- Low height—for safety through low center of gravity.
- Broad width and wide treads—for stability.
- Small turning circle—for easy turning in tight places.
- Light weight per horsepower—for liveliness.

Designed for Functional Beauty

- Sweep-Sight windshield—for maximum forward vision.
- Shallow top and "dip-down" belt line—for large side windows.
- Full wraparound rear window—for "see-through" vision.
- Low hood and rear deck—for a better view of the road.
- Four-fender visibility—for easier car guidance.
- Hooded headlights, high and widely spaced to mark car width.
- Smart hood ornament and hood emblem.
- Large lattice radiator grille—for efficient engine cooling.
- Sturdy contoured wraparound bumpers—for maximum protection.
- Straight-through sides, inswept at top and bottom—to reduce rubbing.
- Protective chrome—to prevent damage to finish.
- Concealed fuel filler—for smarter appearance.
- Solid door handles protecting pushbutton releases.
- Broadly spaced and high tail lights—for car-width demarcation.

A NEW CONCEPT OF THE LOW-COST CAR!

STYLE...A COMBINATION OF SIZE AND SHAPE

There is no car quite like the Motoramic Chevrolet. It stands out among all cars because of its unique combination of liveliness and functional beauty.

In styling any car, its size must be established before it is shaped and decorated. In a car of Chevrolet's class, size plays an even more important role in styling than in more expensive cars. The car should be big inside for comfort, yet small outside for easy handling in modern-day traffic. In the Motoramic Chevrolet, that goal has been reached—with outstanding success. Not only is this new car bigger inside and smaller outside, but *it looks much longer*.

This results from compactness in design. To use the sedans as an example, compactness in the sides broadens the car interior by approximately two inches, providing more room at hat, shoulder, and hip levels. At the same time, it decreases the car width by one inch. Redesign of the body and chassis lowers the body, reducing the over-all car height by

2½ inches for a better appearance—and also lowers the hood and rear deck 3½ inches, making the road immediately ahead and behind the car easier to see. Compactness ahead of the front wheels reduces the overhang approximately two inches, providing a steeper ramp angle. This reduction, and an added inch of trunk-room behind the rear wheels, result in a car length that is approximately one inch shorter —with no change in wheelbase.

To make the car look longer and more massive, the fenders are kept at the 1954 level but are lengthened, making all four of them visible from the driver's seat to serve as guides in maneuvering the car.

For greater stability, not only is the car's center of gravity lower, but also the 115-inch wheelbase is relatively longer, because of the shorter car length, and the wheel treads are relatively broader, due to the narrower car width and the widening of the front tread to nearly equal the broad rear tread.

Compactness in design also is responsible for the elimination of unnecessary weight. With great increases in horsepower, this results in a power-to-weight ratio that is enviably high, making the Motoramic Chevrolet one of the most lively performers on the road.

SIZE . . . THE LONG AND SHORT OF IT

Except for the wheelbase and rear tread, every major dimension of the Motoramic Chevrolet is new, giving a completely new size to this wonderful new car—a size that makes it bigger inside yet smaller outside.

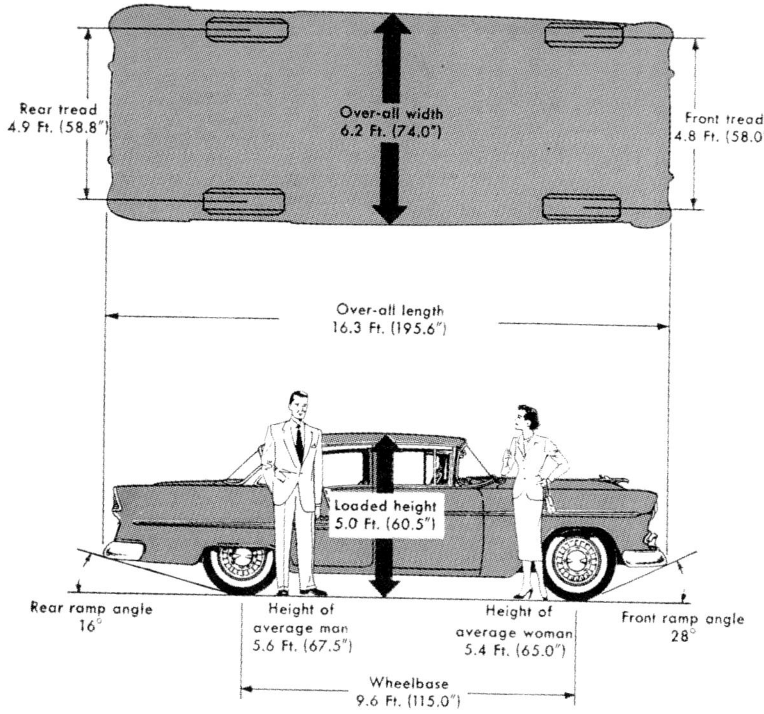

SEDAN DIMENSIONS EXPRESSED IN FEET
FOR EASIEST UNDERSTANDING

But size is relative and can be appreciated only by comparison. The Motoramic Chevrolet has size advantages over every other car—whether it is in the low-, medium-, or high-price class. And, by comparing Chevrolet with any other car—dimension by dimension—the salesman can point out these advantages to good effect. For example, even when compared with a comparable model of one of the most expensive makes of car, a car that costs 2½ times as much, the least expensive Chevrolet shows up well.

HOW BIG IS BIG?

(For interpretation, see next page.)

		"One-Fifty" 4-Door Sedan	Car Costing 2½ Times as Much	Difference (at extra cost)
ROOM	Front Seat—			
	Head room	35.7"	35.8"	+ 0.1"
	Shoulder room	56.8"	59.4"	+ 2.6"
	Hip room	62.0"	64.3"	+ 2.3"
	Leg room	43.1"	43.3"	+ 0.2"
	Rear Seat—			
	Head room	35.4"	35.6"	+ 0.2"
	Shoulder room	56.4"	58.9"	+ 2.5"
	Hip room	63.0"	65.2"	+ 2.2"
	Leg room	40.8"	46.3"	+ 5.5"
OVER-ALL SIZE	Length	16.3 ft.	18.9 ft.	+ 2.6 ft.
	Width	6.2 ft.	6.7 ft.	+ 0.5 ft.
	Height	5.0 ft.	5.2 ft.	+ 0.2 ft.
SUPPORT	Wheelbase	115.0"	133.0"	+18.0"
	Front tread	58.0"	60.0"	+ 2.0"
	Rear tread	58.8"	63.1"	+ 4.3"
HANDLING	Turning dia.	38.0 ft.	45.0 ft.	+ 7.0 ft.
	Front ramp angle	28.0 deg.	19.9 deg.	− 8.1 deg.
	Rear ramp angle	16.0 deg.	11.8 deg.	− 4.2 deg.
LIVELINESS	Dry weight	3135 lb.	4540 lb.	+1405 lb.
	V8 horsepower	180 h.p.	250 h.p.	+ 70 h.p.
	H.P. per lb.	.057 h.p.	.055 h.p.	− .002 h.p.
BRAKING	Brake dia.	11"	12"	+1"
	Lb. per inch dia.	285	378	+93 lb.

(Continued from page 53)

TURNING

The Chevrolet can make a complete turn in a street that is much too narrow (by 7 feet) for the big car to turn in.

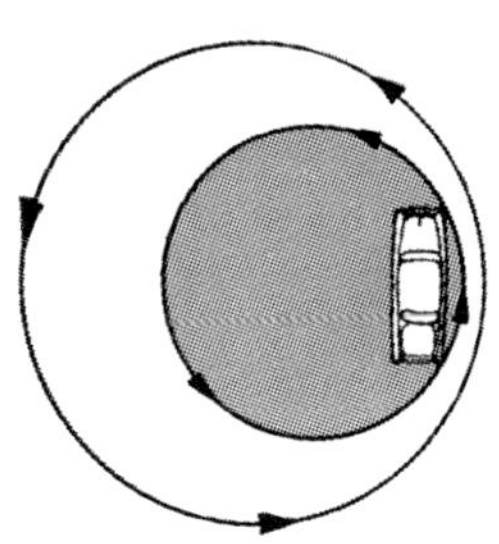

LENGTH

The Chevrolet fits in garages that are too small for the big car and can be parked in spaces that are too short for the big car. Maneuvering in traffic or on the highway also is easier with the Chevrolet.

ROOM

The Chevrolet matches the big car in head room and front-seat leg room. Otherwise, the big car is about 2¼ inches wider (at about $1300 per inch) and has somewhat more rear-seat leg room. When it is considered that usually only one to four persons ride in a car, this big-car characteristic loses value.

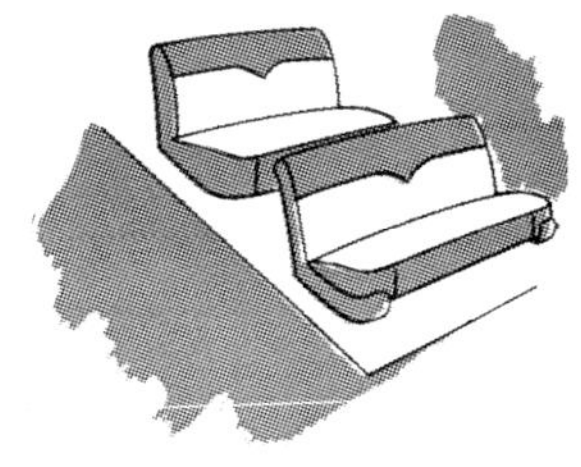

Style

RAMPS

The Chevrolet can go up drive-way ramps and other short inclines and can come down slopes that the big car would scrape.

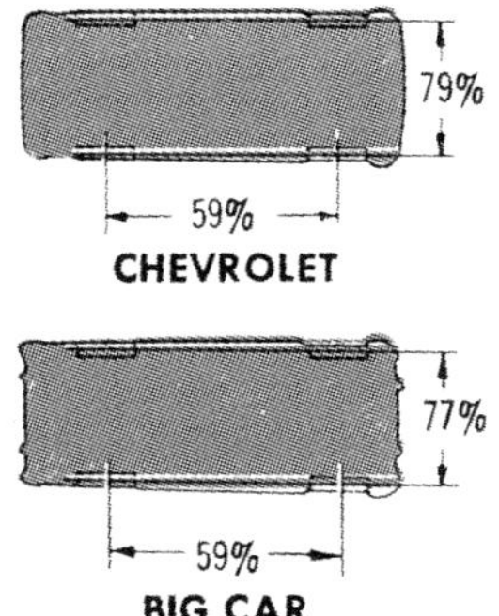

STABILITY

The Chevrolet wheelbase is as long in relation to car length as that of the big car and its tread is broader in relation to car width. Moreover, Chevrolet's nearly equal treads, front and rear, provide better tracking.

Chevrolet—Tread 79%   W. B. 59%
Big Car—Tread 77%   W. B. 59%

PERFORMANCE

With the same kind of engine (V8 with dual exhaust system) as the big car, the Chevrolet's power-to-weight ratio is better than that of the big car, indicating that it will perform better. For stopping, Chevrolet's brakes are larger in relation to car weight. And, for economy, the Chevrolet costs less to buy, operate, and maintain.

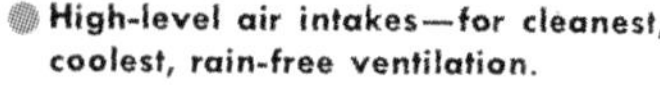

- Sweep-Sight windshield—for maximum vision.

- High-level air intakes—for cleanest, coolest, rain-free ventilation.

- Low hood—for better view of road.

- Headlight hoods—to direct beams and shield lights from rain and snow.

- Large parking lights, widely spaced like headlights—to denote car width at night.

- Large radiator grille—for efficient engine cooling.

- Full wraparound rear window—for "see through" vision.

- Low rear deck—for better view of road.

- Long, high-crowned fenders, all visible from driver's seat.

- Extra-large rear lights—widely spaced to mark car width at night.

- Extra-low trunk sill—for easiest loading of trunk.

- Easy-to-lift trunk handle—combined with rear emblem for best appearance.

- Protected license plate—illuminated by lights in bumper guards.

- Guards between bumpers and body —to protect body from stones and splash.

- Large chrome wheel disks or hub caps.

- Lustrous, durable, pyroxylin lacquer finish—for longer-lasting beauty.

Style

- Crank-operated ventipanes—for No-Draft ventilation.

- Extra-large side windows with "dip-down" belt line.

- Fuel filler, high for accessibility, concealed for best appearance.

- Straight-through sides, inswept at top and bottom—to minimize area that might be rubbed.

- Protective chrome moldings—to prevent damage to finish.

- Solid door handles—shaped to shield pushbuttons.

- Sturdy bumpers with anti-lock guards—for maximum protection.

- Flanged wheel openings—for greatest strength.

BEAUTY . . . with a PURPOSE in EVERY DETAIL!

Style

STYLING with a NEW "LOOK"

NEW PANORAMIC VISIBILITY

More glass area, all around the car, results from lowering the hood, belt line, and rear deck one inch more than the top was lowered. In four-door sedans, for example, there are increases of 165 square inches in the windshield, 189 in the side windows, and 187 in the rear window—a total of 541 square inches, or more than 18 per cent—to make motoring more enjoyable and safer.

NEW SWEEP-SIGHT WINDSHIELD

The new windshield curves in one continuous sweep into the body sides, where it meets vertical pillars that set back beyond the driver's normal range of

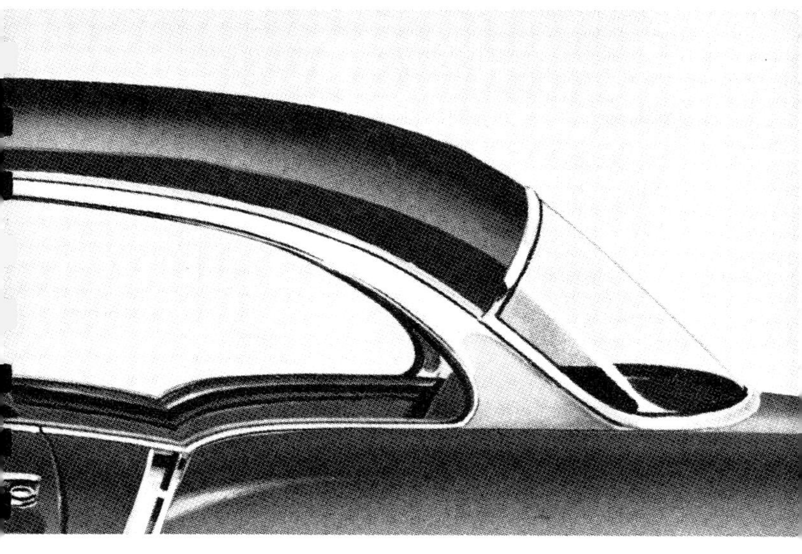

... for a NEW "OUTLOOK"

forward vision. Windshield openings are similar for all models. However, in the Bel Air Sport Coupe and Convertible, which have lower tops, the windshield height is somewhat less than in other models.

LARGE WINDOW AREAS (in square feet)

BODY TYPE	Wind-shield	Side Windows	Rear Window	All Around
4-Door Sedan	7.1	9.9	7.4	24.4
2-Door Sedan	7.1	10.2	7.4	24.7
Club Coupe	7.1	10.2	7.4	24.7
Utility Sedan	7.1	10.1	7.4	24.6
Sport Coupe	6.8	9.0	7.3	23.1
Convertible	6.8	8.1	4.8	19.7
4-Door Station Wagon	7.1	16.7	3.8	27.6
2-Door Station Wagon	7.1	17.1	3.8	28.0

NEW NO-DRAFT VENTIPANES

The new rectangular ventipanes are operated by crank regulators that are exclusive to Chevrolet in its field. The ventipanes can be opened to introduce draft-free air into the car, or even may be reversed to scoop in great quantities of air. Spring-loaded bolts latch them securely to vertical pillars built into the doors. Metal frames protect the edges of the glass. Similar frames protect the door and rear-quarter windows of the Sport Coupe and Convertible.

NEW SIDE WINDOWS

All crank-operated side windows open fully. For the greatest convenience, optional electric-power window lifts lower and raise these windows automatically. Stationary rear-quarter windows in four-door sedans provide extra vision for rear seat occupants, while the stationary rear-quarter windows of Chevrolet's new station wagons wrap around the rear corners to meet the end gates. Both types are exclusive to Chevrolet in its field. In all sedans and coupes, a "dip-down" belt line adds a touch of distinction that is found in no other low-priced car.

NEW REAR WINDOWS

Full wraparound rear windows, in all sedans and the Sport Coupe and Club Coupe, not only provide more "looking out" area but also allow the driver of a following car to see completely through a Motoramic Chevrolet so that he may observe traffic changes ahead—promoting his own safety and that of the Chevrolet's passengers. Similar results are obtained with a large vinyl plastic window in the Bel Air Convertible and a large curved window in each of the station wagons.

THOROUGH SEALING OF ALL WINDOWS

Every Chevrolet window pane is thoroughly sealed to insure the comfort of passengers and prevent water leakage that might damage the car's interior. All stationary windows are permanently sealed in rubber; compressed rubber seals are used around the ventipanes; and other windows that open slide in rubber-backed fabric-lined glass-run channels, and have rubber seals at their sills, both inside and outside the glass.

The occupants of Chevrolets are well protected from glass breakage by the provision of high-quality safety glass in every window pane. Two kinds are used, depending on the shape and size of the window. The solid type breaks only under terrific impact, into small, blunt-edged, harmless chunks. The laminated type consists of a sandwich of two glass panes that are bonded together by tough, transparent, blister-proof plastic. This type may be crushed, rolled, and warped, but the glass particles still will adhere to the plastic.

For the best driving vision, the windshield, ventipanes, and all glass rear windows are made of the highest-quality ground and polished safety plate glass.

OPTIONAL TINTED SAFETY PLATE GLASS

For those who drive a great deal in glaring sunlight, E-Z-Eye safety plate glass is a boon. Its bluish-green tint reduces sun glare and heat materially for more comfortable driving. The windshield, in this option, is available either with or without a darker shaded band across the top that further increases driver eye comfort. Also, the standard windshield may be fitted with a transparent green plastic glare shield that is available as an accessory.

NEW . . . WHEN COMING!

The immediate impression of the Motoramic Chevrolet is one of fresh new beauty—in exquisite taste. Here is beauty that is new, practical, and distinctive, with none of the non-functional effects that soon may outdate other cars in Chevrolet's price class. Not only does the new Chevrolet look like a big car but in every line and detail it reflects the high quality usually found only in big cars.

NEW FRONT APPEARANCE

As viewed from the front, the car appears much more massive and stable. This is due to the lower heights of the body and hood, which concentrate more of the car's mass below the belt line, and to the massiveness imparted by every component.

The lower and wider hood blends more gracefully with the fenders and slopes sharply downward to meet the radiator grille. Now formed from one sheet of steel, it presents a smooth surface that is decorated by an attractive rib at the center, a new ornament with an eagle motif, and a colorful new plastic emblem that is broader to contribute to the accent on massiveness. The top of the radiator grille frame is attached to and lifts with the hood when it is opened. Because the hood opening is larger and lower, access to the engine for servicing is easier.

NEW LATTICE RADIATOR GRILLE

Corvette influence is apparent in the rectangular frame of the radiator grille, but the actual grille-work is composed of many narrow bars in a lattice pattern. By this arrangement, the "gaping mouth" appearance found in other cars is avoided, the radiator is completely hidden, and the flow of air to the radiator assures efficient engine cooling.

Distinctive hoods crown the Chevrolet headlights. Unlike other hoods that are just parts of the light rims, these are gracefully formed in the fenders. Beyond the beauty they add to the car, they help direct the light rays and shield the lights from snow and drippings that might ice the glass. Similar styling is found in the parking lights.

NEW WRAPAROUND FRONT BUMPER

The sturdy new bumper is shaped to the new front-end contour. At its sides, where it curves around the fenders, it is deeper to afford more corner protection. The well-spaced bumper guards have projecting tops that help prevent bumper locking. Available as accessories, fender guards that are mounted on top of the bumper ends, and a radiator grille guard that spans the space between the bumper guards, further emphasize the massive front appearance. To help keep the front of the car clean and to protect it from damage by gravel, a horizontal splash-and-gravel guard is formed in the base of the sheet metal just behind the bumper.

NEW FRONT CHROME

The strikingly beautiful front end of every Chevrolet is accented by decorative and protective chrome. This includes the hood ornament and emblem frame, headlight rims and parking light frames, the entire radiator grille, and the bumpers and guards. And, on Bel Air and "Two-Ten" models, a chrome reveal frames the windshield. Typical of the high quality so evident in Chevrolet is the chrome plating of the back of the Bel Air rearview mirror.

From the side, every beautiful new Chevrolet conveys an impression of greater length and fleetness. In the sedans and coupes, this results from the lowering of the car's top contour, including hood, body, and rear deck, and the lengthening of both front and rear fenders to nearly bumper length.

DISTINCTIVE NEW SIDE TREATMENT

Whereas the belt lines of competitive cars are flat, that of Chevrolet is distinguished by the convergence of the high front and rear fender crowns in a pronounced "dip-down" in the rear quarter of the body. Another distinguishing note is the windsplit that is formed in the front fender as a continuation of the headlight hood. Still another is the strengthening lip that completely frames the front wheel opening, and continues along the body sill to reinforce the rear wheel opening. To make these points outstanding, the car's sides are simple in contour with an inward curvature at the belt and sill.

Style

NEW SIDE CHROME

The smart beauty of "One-Fifty" models is kept simple, with chrome only in the Chevrolet name on the front fender, the ventipane frame, door handles, and hub caps. On "Two-Ten" models, however, the "dip-down" is high-lighted by chrome window sill, sash, and rear fender moldings. And, on Bel Air models, full emphasis is given to the points of interest by chrome on the front fender windsplit, a broader rear fender molding with a Winter White center, the Bel Air name and gold-plated crest at the juncture of the sash and rear fender moldings, a molding that frames the window group, and by full-size chrome wheel disks. In these models, too, smartness in detail is noticeable in the provision of chrome on the windshield pillar and between the rear quarter and rear windows.

Chrome accessories that embellish and protect the sides of Chevrolets include front fender stone guards, body sill moldings, door handle shields, door edge guards, and a guard that prevents chipping of the finish around the gasoline tank filler door opening.

NEW . . . WHEN GOING!

Like the beautiful front end of the car, the rear of
every new Chevrolet sedan and coupe appears
broader and more stable, because of the greater
emphasis that is given to the car's width by the
lower body top and rear deck.

NEW REAR DECK

The lower and longer deck, level with the fenders
just behind the rear window, slopes slightly downward between the fenders, adding length to the
fender crowns. The deck lid is much broader and
extends down nearly to bumper level so that, when
it is open, there is ease of access to the luggage
compartment. To accent the deck width, the lid
handle, with its colorful emblem, is extra-broad.

The fenders jut farther to the rear and terminate in attractive lights that accentuate the fender length. Below the lights, "pedestals" carry the fender lines down to bumper level.

NEW WRAPAROUND REAR BUMPER

The massive bumper follows the deck contour and wraps around into the car sides. To prevent "hooking," its ends are inset in the fenders and its guards are shaped to prevent bumper locking. Accessory fender guards add to the corner protection. Protection of the deck from splash is provided by a ledge that juts from the body to the bumper. Rubber, compressed between the two, makes a water- and dirt-proof seal.

NEW REAR CHROME

Sparkle is added to the rear of every Chevrolet by the chrome bumpers and light and emblem frames. And, on Bel Air and "Two-Ten" sedans and coupes, the rear window, too, is framed in chrome. To enhance the Convertible, a chrome molding decorates the inside of the windshield. An accessory chrome frame adjusts to fit the license plate. In addition, every Chevrolet V8 is identified by chrome "V" medallions on the rear fender pedestals.

NEW "CONTINENTAL" WHEEL CARRIER

To increase trunk space and give the car the extra-long Continental sports-car look, an accessory wheel carrier and special rear bumper are available for all sedans and coupes. The wheel, with its metal cover, is mounted vertically behind the rear deck within an offset in the bumper. For access to the trunk, it can be lowered to a horizontal position.

A NEW STYLE IN STATION WAGONS

The completely new and different styling of the Chevrolet station wagons outdates the best efforts of competitive car makers. Not only are these cars fully six inches lower than before, giving them an appearance of great length and swiftness, but their upper structure is one unique wall of glass that circumscribes the car. Segmented only by the narrow pillars that unite the Turret Top and the body proper, this wall is composed of the new Sweep-Sight windshield, new side and rear windows, and wraparound rear-quarter windows that are exclusive to Chevrolet in its field.

At the rear, the body slopes gracefully between the jutting fenders down to the bumper. The large tail lights in the fenders and the license plate, indented in the bumper, are clearly visible with the tail gate down. Chrome decoration, series by series, parallels that of the new Chevrolet sedans and coupes. In the Bel Air and "Two-Ten" models, the windows are accentuated by distinctive chrome top and belt moldings that extend around the sides and rear.

BEAUTY IN A FINISH THAT LASTS

Every Chevrolet is finished with the same high-quality polished lacquer finish that is offered on America's most expensive cars. There is no finer finish on the market. When compared with the synthetic enamel finishes used on competitive cars, the Chevrolet finish is outstanding in every respect. It is smooth and uniform, without the "orange peel" surface of the other finishes. It has greater richness and depth. (Even after neglect, its gloss can be restored to its original luster by polishing.) And, if repairs must be made, they can be made better and more easily. In fact, a Chevrolet owner can obtain a small jar of exactly the same lacquer as on his car from his dealer and make small touch-ups himself.

RICH, BEAUTIFUL COLORAMIC STYLING

- Color-keyed, two-tone treatments.
- Well-tailored, high-quality fabrics and vinyls.
- Tasteful chrome decoration.
- Good-looking, durable floor coverings.

GRACEFUL INSTRUMENT PANEL

- Matching instrument cluster and radio speaker.
- Central glove compartment with lock—and light.*
- Built-in ash receptacle*, cigaret lighter*, clock*.
- Easy-to-read instruments; at-hand controls.
- Attractive steering wheel; concentric column.
- Choice of three accessory radios.

WIDE, FORM-FITTING SEATS

- Resilient, well-padded seat construction.
- Foam rubber cushions in seat and arm rests.*
- Inclined-plane seat adjustment; power option.
- Center-fold two-door-model front-seat back rests.
- Swing-out front door hinges; positive door checks.

EXCELLENT VISION AND VENTILATION

- Large, high-quality, safety glass windows.
- Automatic* and panel-controlled interior lighting.
- Crank-operated ventipanes and windows;
  optional power-lifts.
- High-level ventilation; optional air conditioning.
- De luxe or recirculating accessory heaters.

MASTER-KEY LOCK OPERATION

- Pushbutton lock releases in door handles.
- Keyless door locking; one key fits all car locks.

LARGE LUGGAGE SPACE

- Low-sill trunk with key-release and slam lock.
- Convenient parcel shelf in sedans and coupes.
- Spacious load compartments in station wagons.
- Quick-folding station wagon rear seat.

*In Two-Ten and/or Bel Air Models.

BEAUTY—COMFORT—CONVENIENCE . . .
MATCHED ONLY IN COSTLIER CARS!

COMFORT . . .
WITH BEAUTY

The luxurious sitting-room comfort, modern-living convenience, and tasteful beauty inside the Motoramic Chevrolet exceed the greatest expectations.

NEW COLORAMIC STYLING

Nowhere is the spirit of the new car captured better than in its lovely and gracious two-tone interiors—color-keyed with the exteriors, in Bel Air and "Two-Ten" models, for an outdoor living-room effect.

TRADITIONAL BODY-BY-FISHER QUALITY

Striking in every model are the fine quality, craftsmanship, and style for which "Body by Fisher" is famous. No other make of body is so well known for careful attention to detail and consideration for comfort; no other approaches Fisher's traditional excellence. Fisher bodies grace the finest cars on the road, are *exclusive* to Chevrolet in its field!

Luxurious and colorful materials in the new Chevrolet are offered in *30* distinctive combinations. Exciting new colors and patterns are combined in materials that are not only beautiful, but tough and long-lasting. Every material has passed rigid tests for fade and wear resistance. The smart new fabrics come in a variety of patterns and colors that give a feeling of richness and quality. Beautifully grained vinyls are used on side walls and seat risers; a special form-fitting vinyl assures smooth, comfortable seat cushions. In Bel Air and "Two-Ten" models, chrome moldings accent the tailored side walls and front seat end panels.

NEW ROOMINESS

In the past, Chevrolet head room and front-seat leg room have equalled those of otherwise larger cars. Now, large increases in width—in hat room, shoulder room, and hip room—give the Motoramic Chevrolet enviable sitting space, in both front and rear seats.

NEW CONVENIENCE

For convenience, model for model, no car in its field has ever equalled Chevrolet. But, for 1955, Chevrolet provides even greater convenience with the introduction, *in standard, accessory, and optional equipment,* of the many new features described on the following pages.

A NEW KIND OF LOW-COST CAR

In short, everything possible has been done, stylewise and design-wise, to make the Motoramic Chevrolet as comfortable, beautiful, and convenient inside as it is new and striking outside. It is truly a new kind of low-cost car . . . rivaling the most expensive in luxury.

Interiors

BEL AIR
SPORT COUPE

New straw pattern cloth and leather-grained vinyl, in straw with red, blue, turquoise, or green, or coral and gray. Harmonious carpets.

"TWO-TEN"
DELRAY
CLUB COUPE

All-vinyl interior, in green and beige, blue and beige, or black and ivory. Harmonious carpets.

"TWO-TEN"
SEDAN

Beautiful, nylon-faced fabric, ripple-weave gabardine, and leather-grained vinyl, in two-tone green, blue, or brown. Colored rubber floor mats.

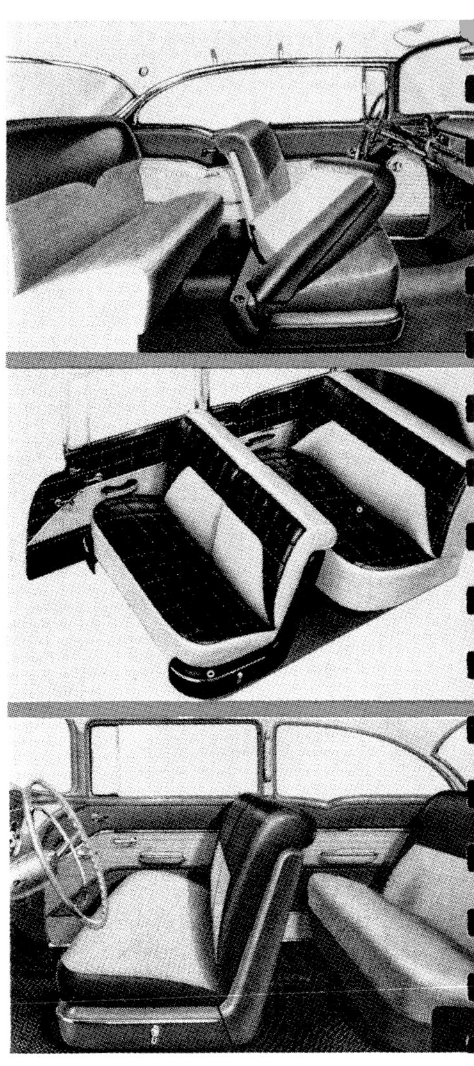

BEL AIR SEDAN

Pattern cloth, gabardine, and vinyl, in two-tone blue or green, beige and brown, ivory and turquoise, coral and gray. Harmonious carpets.

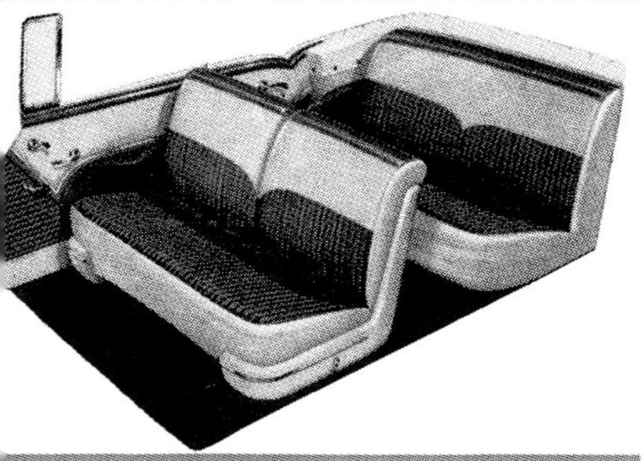

BEL AIR CONVERTIBLE

All-vinyl interior, in two-tone green or blue, beige with red or brown, ivory and turquoise, coral and gray. Harmonious carpets, and fabric top in green, blue, beige, or vinylized white.

"ONE-FIFTY" SEDAN

Gray chevron-pattern cloth, with black vinyl trim. Black rubber floor mats.

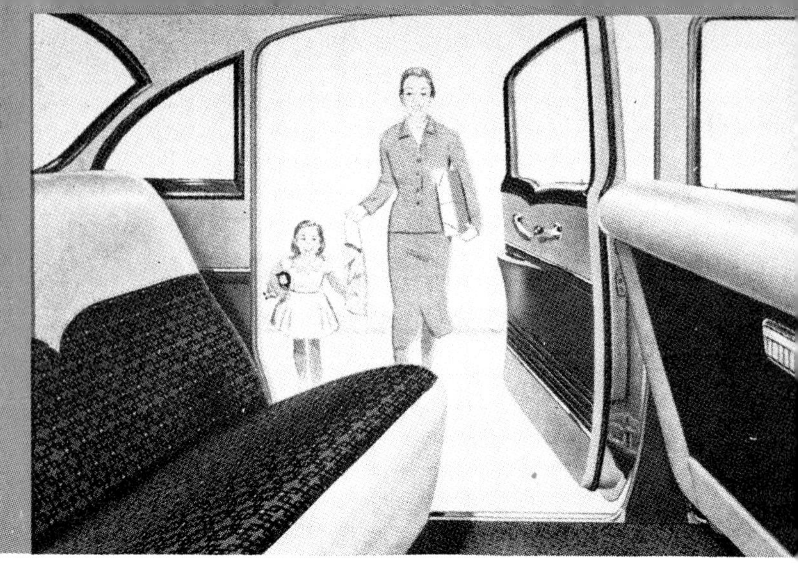

All doors are hinged at the front for safety, and open wide for easy access to the inviting interior. Offset hinges actually move the front doors out of the way to increase entrance room. Positive checks hold the doors wide open until they are shut intentionally. Decorative plates of etched aluminum protect the door sills from scuffing. New rotary latches permit the doors to close more easily and quietly, and hold them securely shut. Even if a door is not completely closed, it will not open, because teeth of its rotary latch act as safety catches. And, new and exclusive to Chevrolet in its field, the rubber door seals are secured to the doors by many metal clips, in addition to rubber cement, to prevent loosening and to help make door closing easier.

MASTER-KEY AND PUSHBUTTON DOOR LOCK CONTROL

There's no fumbling with keys, because one key operates all car locks. The weather seals of the door and trunk locks don't have to be pushed aside in order to insert the key. Instead, simple insertion or removal of the key automatically causes the seal to uncover or cover the keyhole. The pushbutton door lock releases, shielded from snow and drippings by the solidly mounted door handles, operate easily.

Button-on-sill inside latches are provided for every door and those on the rear doors are "baby-proof"— the doors won't open as long as the buttons are kept pressed down. However, a simple adjustment by the dealer permits the lock to be released by the inside door lever, as on the front doors. When all the buttons are down, the car can be locked from outside— without the key—simply by pushing the outside pushbutton in as the last door is shut—a great convenience when a person is burdened with parcels.

When leaving the car in a parking lot, a special position in the starter-ignition switch permits operation of the car by the lot attendants without the use of the key. This permits the driver to take the key with him so the contents of his locked glove compartment and trunk will be safer.

Every key has a number for identification, so the owner can order duplicates. But the number is on a tab that is removable, making it impossible for thieves, who may have key sets, to identify the key.

NEW AUTOMATIC INSIDE LIGHTS

When any door on the Bel Air model or either front door of a "Two-Ten" model, is opened, the inside light goes on automatically and stays on until the door is closed. In addition, the light of every model may be turned on or off easily by simply turning the main light switch on the instrument panel. In all models, except the Sport Coupe and Convertible, there is a central dome light. Attractively framed in chrome, its circular lens is plastic instead of glass to lessen the possibility of breakage. A similar, but smaller light is provided in each rear corner of the Sport Coupe. In the Convertible, there are two courtesy lights, underneath the instrument panel, that also are available as accessories in other models.

NEW BROADER SEATS

All seats are lower, because the bodies are lower, and all front seats, and the rear seats of four-door models, are right beside the doors. So, to enter, all one does is sit down and swing his feet in. All seats are wider. Seat widths of sedans, for example, now average 5 feet 2½ inches. The seat frames are sturdy steel structures with resilient, S-wire springs that provide lasting uniform body support. Unlike coil springs, they allow plenty of room below the front seat that is used to provide more foot room for rear

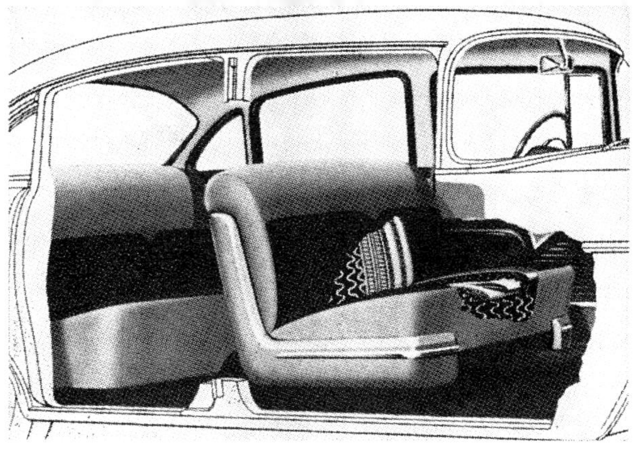

seat occupants and the passage of air to the rear seat. Comfortable, firm seat padding makes sitting in a Motoramic Chevrolet like sitting in one's easy chair. And the front-seat cushions of Bel Air and "Two-Ten" models and the rear-seat cushions of Bel Air sedans and coupes have foam rubber pads for even more comfort.

CENTER-FOLD BACK RESTS

For the greatest ease of access to the rear seat (or load compartment) two-door models feature center-fold front-seat back rests. Each half of the back rest is hinged so it tilts inward and out of the way as it is folded forward. Entering or leaving the rear seat of Bel Air and "Two-Ten" two-door sedans and the Club Coupe is facilitated by assist straps.

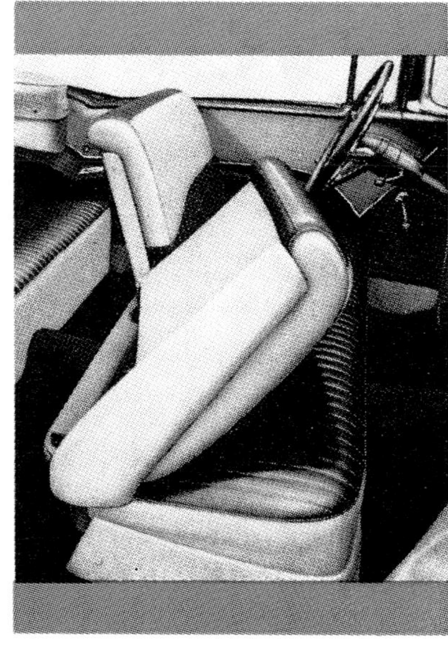

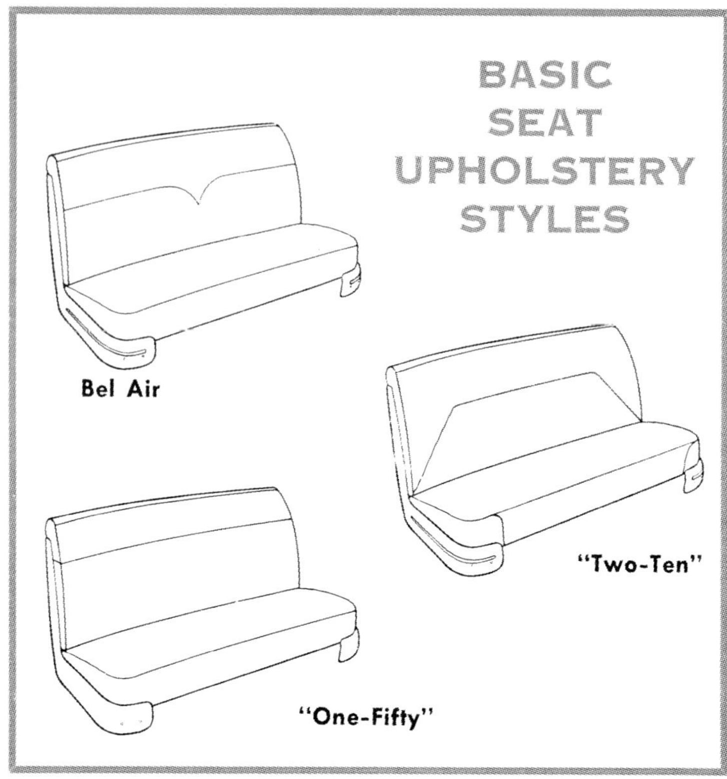

NEW SEAT UPHOLSTERY STYLES

The beautiful new seat upholstery (described on pages 75-77) is provided in three basic styles, one for each series, as illustrated.

ACCESSORY SEAT COVERS

For those who wish to preserve the original upholstery, there are accessory seat cushion covers of transparent nylon-dacron, in six different colors, for four-door and two-door sedans and the Sport Coupe. Also there are accessory sets of seat and back rest covers in plastic, nylon, or fiber—in blue, brown, or green—for four-door and two-door sedans.

EASY FRONT-SEAT ADJUSTMENT

The spring-assisted inclined-plane front-seat adjustment permits the seat to be moved forward and up
or backward and down with pushbutton ease. The
adjustment range is large, so that nearly every driver,
whether short or tall, is assured of a comfortable
driving position. The adjustment control, on the side
of the seat, is easily reached without stooping or
fumbling. For the utmost of ease, an optional electric-
power control adjusts the seat automatically.

COMFORTABLE ARM RESTS

Arm rests are standard equipment for both the front
and the rear seats of sedans and coupes and the
station wagon front seats—in Bel Air and "Two-Ten"
models—and also are available as accessories in
"One-Fifty" models. All are comfortably padded
with foam rubber and surfaced with durable vinyl;
and those on the doors have hand grips that facilitate
door closing. Bel Air arm rests, except in the rear
of two-door sedans, are the smart built-in type used
on more expensive cars. The others are the attractive applied type that features a sturdy plastic base.

Every glass window is attractively framed in metal. In the sedans, most coupes, and the station wagons, lacquered garnish moldings are used. In the Sport Coupe, extra smartness is provided by the chrome edging on all side windows, a chrome rear window garnish molding, and chrome roof rails and bows. And, in the Convertible, chrome not only edges the side windows but also frames the top and sides of the windshield.

EASY WINDOW OPERATION

All windows that open, including the front-door ventipanes, are controlled by easy-turning, positive-acting crank regulators. Crank-operation of the ventipanes eliminates unnecessary tugging to get no-draft ventilation. And the spring-loaded sliding-bolt latches of these panes prevent illegal entry. With Chevrolet's optional power control, quiet electric power instantly goes to work at a finger touch to raise or lower the windows. In addition to a master control at the driver's window, there are individual window controls so that each passenger can adjust his window quickly, simply, automatically.

LOW-HUB HARDWARE

All window and ventipane regulators and door remote control levers are shaped and located for easiest operation. Their low hubs place them close to the side walls so they are less likely to catch on clothing. Designed by master craftsmen and finished in chrome with black plastic knobs, they reflect the best of taste.

COMFORTABLE FLOORS

Like the toe panel of the front seat, the rear-seat footrest is formed in the steel floor for firmest support, and both are inclined at comfortable angles. Because the pedals are now the suspended type, the floor has no holes of any kind that might permit water or dirt to enter. Thick jute insulation is covered by easily cleaned, durable rubber mats, in "One-Fifty" and "Two-Ten" models and the Bel Air Station Wagon, and by luxurious, deep-pile carpets in the other Bel Air models and also the "Two-Ten" Club Coupe. The black "One-Fifty" mats harmonize with the gray and black interiors of these cars, while the rubber mats and carpets of the other cars are colored in harmony with their two-tone interiors. Individual accessory rubber mats, in red, brown, green, blue, or black, also are available.

ATTRACTIVE SIDE WALLS AND HEADLINING

The side walls of each series are individually styled with attractive panels that are highlighted, in Bel Air and "Two-Ten" models, by chrome moldings. The panels are either grained or textured vinyl, except the center panels of Bel Air sedans, which are gabardine. The carefully tailored headlinings and sun shade coverings of sedans are plain napped cloth. Vinyl hand-holds and edging on the shades prevent soiling of the cloth. All other models have all-vinyl sun shades and all-vinyl headlinings with, of course, the exception of the Convertible top.

AUTOMATIC CONVERTIBLE TOP

The top of the Convertible is made of "chevrolon," a special weather-resistant fabric. Stretched taut on its steel frame, it is clamped tight to the windshield by a central latch. Rubber at the windshield and sides that overhang the windows seal out the weather. The vinyl plastic rear window is zipper-fastened at its sides and top so it may be lowered into the well for breezeway ventilation. A push-pull knob at the instrument panel activates electrically controlled hydraulic mechanisms that automatically lower or raise the top. The top fits snugly in its well and is covered by a taut snapped-on boot. To raise the top automatically, when the car is unattended and raindrops fall, a new electronic device is available as an accessory. The first drops of rain on a moisture-sensitive grid cause the device to activate the top lift mechanism. A safety switch prevents unintentional operation. The top comes in blue, green, beige, or white, to agree with the car's basic color. The white top is vinyl-coated to make it more attractive and easy to clean. The top boot is a vinyl-coated elastic fabric in one of the two colors of the car's interior trim.

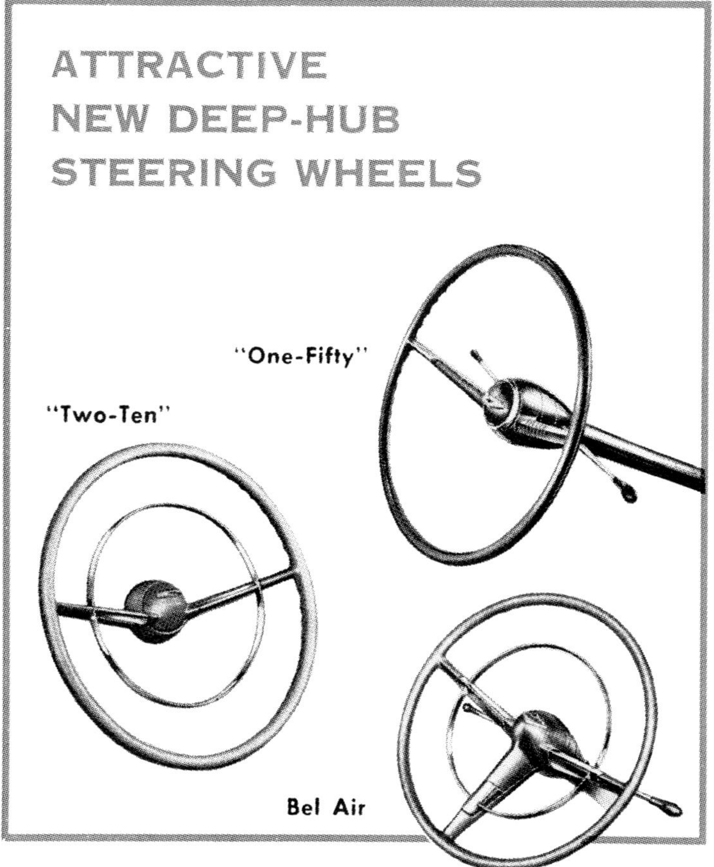

NEW STEERING WHEELS WITH CONCENTRIC COLUMNS

Chevrolet's new steering wheels are all the deep-hub type, with three spokes in Bel Air models, and two in other models. A full-circle horn blowing ring is provided, except in "One-Fifty" models, which have a large horn button. For a neater appearance, the steering column of every Chevrolet now encloses the control mechanisms for both the transmission and direction signals.

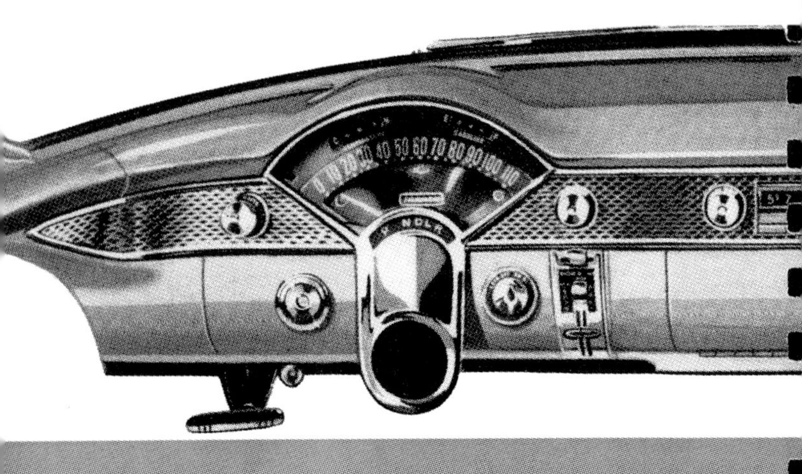

NEW WRAPAROUND INSTRUMENT PANEL

A sense of spaciousness is derived from the larger windshield and the new instrument panel that follows its graceful contour. And a touch of Corvette smartness is found in the hooded quadrant shapes of the instrument cluster and radio speaker. The panel, in Bel Air models, is distinguished by its chrome center panel, the gold-plated "Bel Air" on the speaker, and a handsome electric clock. In other models, the center panel is painted to contrast with the rest of the panel, "Chevrolet" in chrome is on the speaker, and a smart plate provides for installation of the clock as an accessory.

NEW SENSIBLY DESIGNED INSTRUMENT CLUSTER

Unlike the control panels of other low-priced cars, Chevrolet's is designed with every instrument clustered directly in front of the driver for split-second scanning, and with every hand control in easy reach. Even the selector indicator of Powerglide-equipped models is clustered with and lighted with the instruments. And the hood of the cluster minimizes the reflection of instrument lights in the windshield glass.

NEW CENTRAL GLOVE COMPARTMENT

Both driver and passenger benefit from having the glove compartment in the center of the panel, where it is most accessible. The large, fully-lined compartment slants downward so its contents won't fall out when the door is opened. Moreover, the door opens level to serve as a handy shelf. Two circular indentations on this shelf are shaped to hold cups for roadside snacks. The pushbutton keylock is standard equipment and, in Bel Air and "Two-Ten" models, an automatic light is provided.

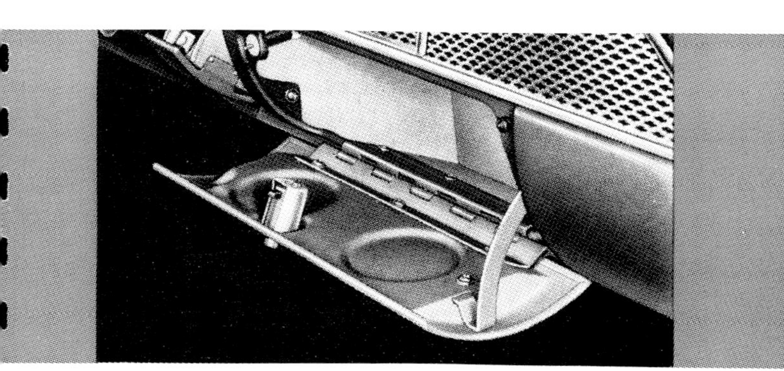

HANDY ACCESSORY TISSUE DISPENSER

A chrome-plated tissue dispenser, which is obtainable as an accessory, mounts directly below the glove compartment. It swivels out, making the tissues handy.

NEW ELECTRIC CLOCK

The new clock used in Bel Air models is also available as an accessory on the other models. It is a self-starting precision timepiece, with a sapphire-jeweled movement, and convenient hand-set knob. Its attractive dial is illuminated.

CONVENIENT SMOKING AIDS

On Bel Air and "Two-Ten" models, a bin-type ash receptacle and pop-out cigaret lighter are convenient to the driver's right hand. The receptacle is concealed in the panel, but opens with a gentle push at its lower edge. Both the receptacle and lighter may be obtained as accessories for "One-Fifty" models. Rear-seat ash receptacles also are provided in Bel Air and "Two-Ten" models. In two-door sedans and coupes, they are built in the arm rests; in four-door sedans, one is inset in the back of the front seat. All ash receptacles have snuffers and are easily lifted out for cleaning.

THREE NEW ACCESSORY RADIOS

The illuminated dial and controls of the radio are centered above the glove compartment. To suit every budget, Chevrolet makes available three types of radios: a 6-tube, hand-tuned receiver, a 7-tube receiver with pushbuttons that are set to the owner's five favorite local stations, and a new 8-tube receiver. In addition to five pushbuttons, this receiver has a signal-seeking feature that is particularly convenient for travellers. When a bar above the dial is pressed repeatedly, the tuner automatically and accurately tunes in, in frequency sequence, the stations of the locality in which the car is travelling.

NEW WEATHER-CONTROL FEATURES

Everything possible has been done to make the occupants of Motoramic Chevrolets comfortable under all weather conditions. Doors and windows completely seal out the elements. Windows open easily for ventilation. After a rain, full length troughs in the roof rails drain the water away so it won't enter open windows, or drip on anyone leaving the car. Thorough insulation, on the cowl and dash, on the floor, within the doors and side walls, and below the top, insulates against heat, cold, and outside noise. And in addition, the Motoramic Chevrolet provides outstanding ventilation, heating, cooling, and air conditioning features, that are unique in its field, to control the "weather" inside the car, as described on the following pages.

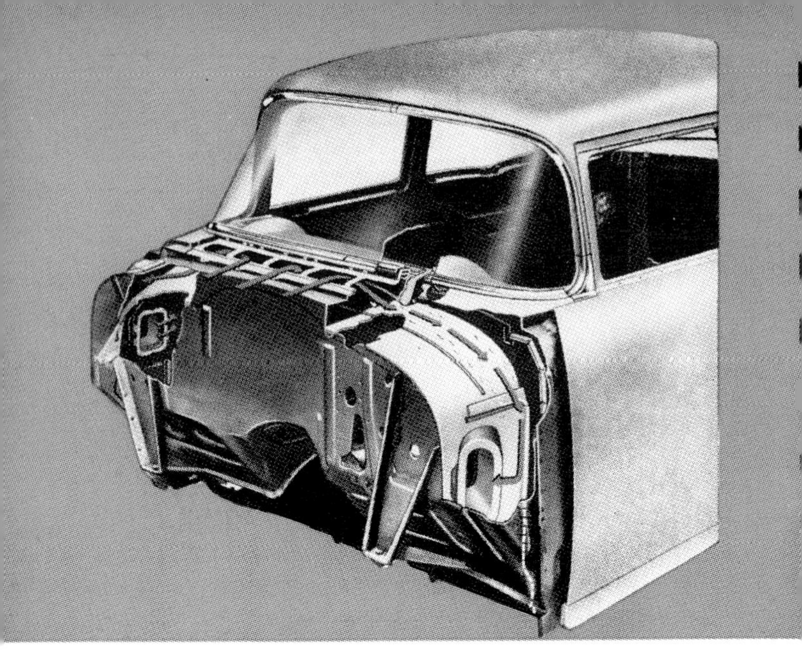

Chevrolet's new ventilation system draws outside air in through a large grille just below the windshield. This high-level air intake maintains a generous supply of cleaner, cooler air because it is located above low-lying road dust and annoying fumes. Before the air enters the car interior, it flows into a large plenum chamber formed by the double walls of the cowl. Any water in it is expelled through drains in the chamber floor. The clean, dry air then enters the interior of the car through two large inlets in the cowl side panels. Each inlet is controlled by a convenient push-pull knob. The design and placement of the inlets allow a large volume of air to circulate throughout the car interior. Air circulation is further aided by the ventipanes in the front door windows. When opened, they permit stale air to be drawn outside while controlled fresh air is constantly provided by the dual inlets. This continual flow of refreshing outside air maintains a more pleasant atmosphere throughout the entire car, and keeps the driver and passengers more comfortable and alert.

Interiors

TWO ACCESSORY HEATER AND DEFROSTER UNITS

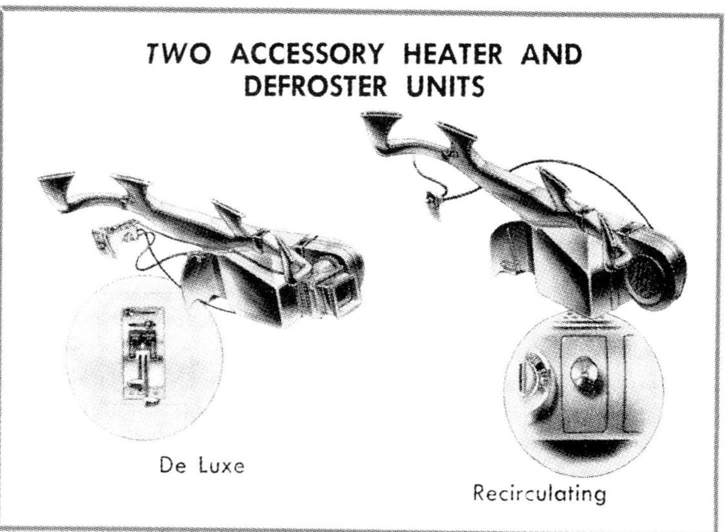

De Luxe

Recirculating

TWO NEW ACCESSORY HEATERS

Two high-capacity heaters, each with a two-speed blower, are available. The simpler one heats the air within the car to the desired degree and keeps it circulating. The De Luxe heater heats and circulates inside air or outside air that it draws from the plenum chamber. The air from either heater enters the interior through a distributor below the instrument panel. Each heater has a defroster manifold with four nozzles that distribute air the full width of the windshield to overcome fogging, frosting, and icing. When operated alone, the blower, like an electric fan, helps make the interior feel cooler. The temperature control knob of the recirculating heater is on the instrument panel beside the ignition switch, and its defroster control is on the heater unit. All controls for the De Luxe heater are included in a lighted chrome-finished panel beside the ignition switch.

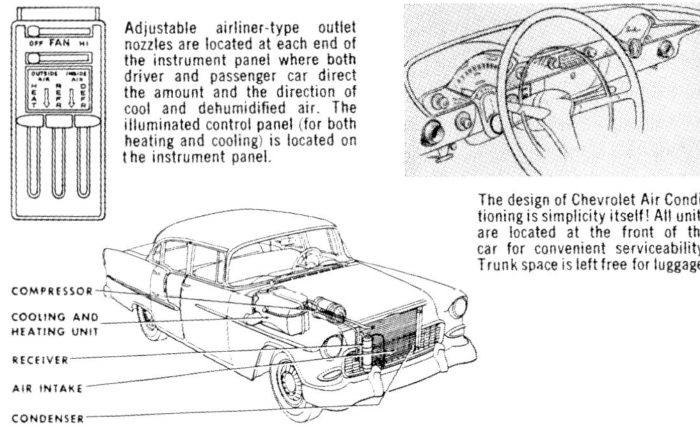

Adjustable airliner-type outlet nozzles are located at each end of the instrument panel where both driver and passenger car direct the amount and the direction of cool and dehumidified air. The illuminated control panel (for both heating and cooling) is located on the instrument panel.

The design of Chevrolet Air Conditioning is simplicity itself! All units are located at the front of the car for convenient serviceability. Trunk space is left free for luggage.

NEW CHEVROLET ALL-WEATHER AIR CONDITIONING BY FRIGIDAIRE

Chevrolet's new air conditioning, (optional in V8 models, except convertible), is a complete weather-control system combined in a single unit. Heating, cooling, and dehumidifying provide controlled comfort throughout the year. Air at the desired temperature enters the car interior through any combination of three inlets—the floor distributor; a pair of adjustable instrument-panel-mounted nozzles; or the defroster slots. Thus either heated or cooled air can be circulated most effectively. Operation is simple—and the main controls are located on the instrument panel just ahead of the driver's right hand.

While Chevrolet's All-Weather Air Conditioning maintains utmost comfort, there are other important benefits, too. Driving is safer, because the driver feels more alert at the wheel. Windows stay closed, which helps keep out bugs, dust, and annoying noises. Traffic is less tiresome, long trips seem shorter, and driver and passengers arrive feeling fresh-looking and neat.

The unit is mounted at the front of the car—with no exposed ducts to mar interior appearance—and no loss of valuable luggage space.

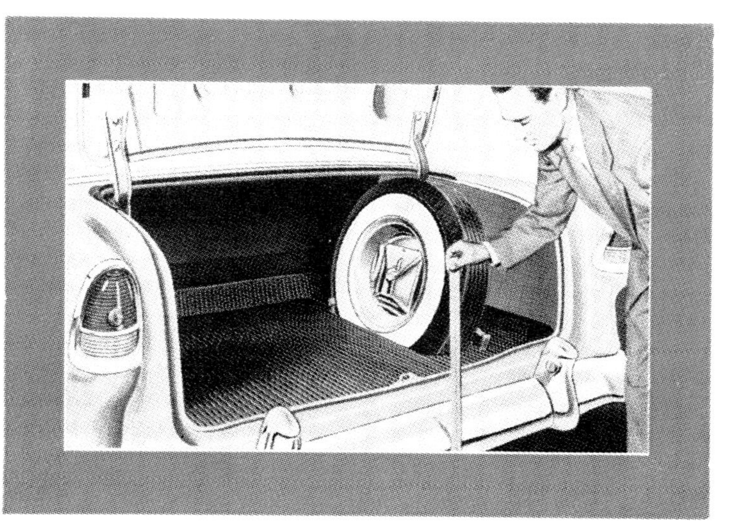

ROOMY LOW-SILL TRUNK

With a twist of the key, the deck lid of sedans and coupes is immediately released. New torsion rods counterbalance the lid, make raising a smooth, one-finger operation. For easiest loading, the sill is exceptionally low, almost level with the trunk floor, and the opening is unusually broad. The trunk itself is spacious, and designed for the efficient stowage of luggage. And the widely spaced hinges are boxed-in so they can't damage the luggage. The jack is cradled in sockets on the wall and floor. The spare wheel is clamped against the jack, while the handle fits in the wheel well. The neat metal side walls are painted the same color as the lower part of the body. The front wall is durable black composition board and the expertly fitted floor mat is black rubber. The deck lid lowers with ease and locks automatically.

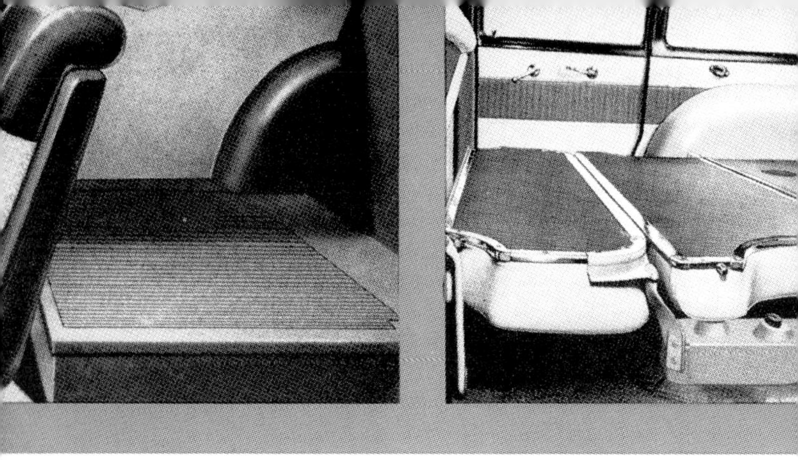

The load compartment is easily reached by folding either half of the seat back rest. The seat back and side walls are finished with tough washable vinyl; the rear wall is rugged composition board; the flat, elevated floor is surfaced with a durable rubber mat. In harmony with the gray and black interior, the whole compartment is black.

CONVENIENT NEW STATION WAGON LOAD COMPARTMENT

All Chevrolet station wagons have a fast-folding rear seat of a new design that adds 10½ inches to the platform length. Both the seat cushion and its back rest fold flat to become part of the platform.

For convenience and down-to-earth utility, the load compartment of the station wagons is outstanding, and in quality of finish it leads the field. Its floor, including the surfaces of the folded seat and the lowered tailgate, is fully covered—with durable ribbed linoleum. And the linoleum is edged with protective chrome, with added chrome around the spare wheel compartment in the Beauville. On the side walls, the vinyl surface is carried through to the rear and, in the Beauville, even covers the wheel houses.

FISHER UNISTEEL BODY STRUCTURE

- Reinforced, all-steel, all-welded, unit construction.
- Solid one-piece Turret Top . . . reinforced at sides, ends, and across its middle.
- Heavily-ribbed full-length floor . . . reinforced by ladder of box section beams.
- Unitized double-walled body sides . . . with fully-panelled double-walled doors.
- Double-walled cowl . . reinforced by integral dash and instrument panels.
- Reinforced box-sectioned door and window pillars.
- Unique mid-body frame . . . comprised of central roof bow, door pillars, and floor cross beam.
- Unitized rear-quarter brace . . . comprised of integrated seat back support and parcel shelf.
- Double-walled deck lid (or end gates).
- Reinforced body-to-frame dash legs.
- Thorough rust-preventive treatment.

UNITIZED FRONT SHEET METAL STRUCTURE

- Rigid one-piece-skirt fender construction.
- Rigid beam fender-to-fender front integration.
- Solid fender-to-cowl rear integration.
- Reinforced single-panel hood.

BOX-GIRDER CHASSIS FRAME

- Box-section side members and front cross member.
- Wide base body-to-frame mounting.
- Solid, corner-braced, bumper-to-frame mountings.

CUSHIONED BODY-TO-FRAME MOUNTINGS

- Rubber-cushioned body mountings.
- Stabilized front sheet metal mounting.

SAFETY THROUGH STRUCTURAL STRENGTH!

STRUCTURE

. . . new strength for safety

There is a sense of serenity in knowing that the Motoramic Chevrolet has been engineered for the utmost in safety—with an entirely new structural design that features completely new, more closely integrated, frame and body structures.

NEW, STRONGER BOX GIRDER CHASSIS FRAME

The frame is 18% lighter, yet 50% more rigid. Its side rails, straighter and with a wider box section that makes them stiffer, now extend from bumper to bumper. The massive front cross member, also of box section, is welded and riveted into the frame structure. The strengthening arch of the double-walled cowl eliminates need for a cross member at the rear of the engine. From there back, the body and frame reinforce one another. The heavy rear cross member is both welded and riveted to the rails. In the Convertible, an X-shaped structure of I-beams that is welded between the rails provides bracing that is given to the other models by the all-steel body top.

Both the front and rear bumpers are solidly bolted to the frame ends and are "corner-braced" by rigid diagonal struts that extend from the frame side rails.

NEW, RUBBER BODY MOUNTS

The body is insulated from the jarring effects of rough roads by live rubber cushions at fourteen mounting points. The cushions are placed at strategic locations to minimize vibrations without impairing the rigidity of the body-frame combination. The freedom of motion between the body and frame that is required to obtain a cushioned ride is slight, so minor frame deflections will cause the body to function as a major reinforcing member of the car structure.

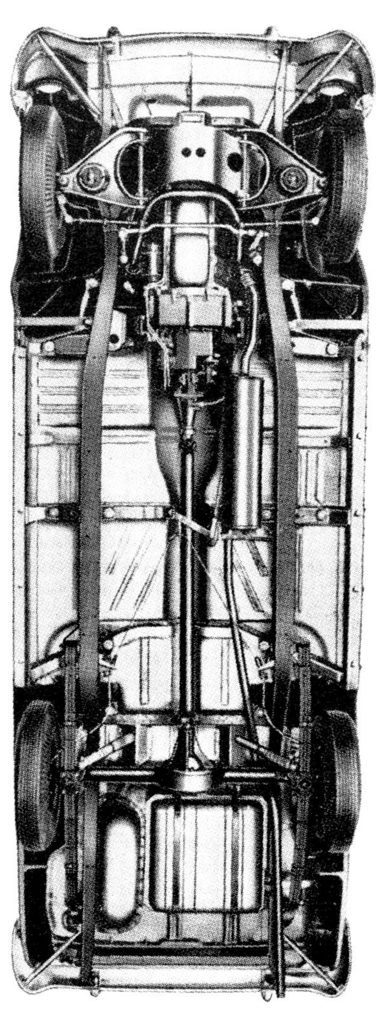

NEW UNISTEEL BODY
. . . by *FISHER!*

SOLID STEEL TOP . . . Reinforced by box-section windshield header, channelled rear window header, field-exclusive center roof bow, and box section roof rails

FULL-LENGTH SOLID STEEL FLOOR . . . Reinforced by integral ribs and ladder of box-sectioned side sills and cross beams

REINFORCED DASH LEGS

DOUBLE-WALLED COWL . . . Reinforced by integral dash and instrument panels

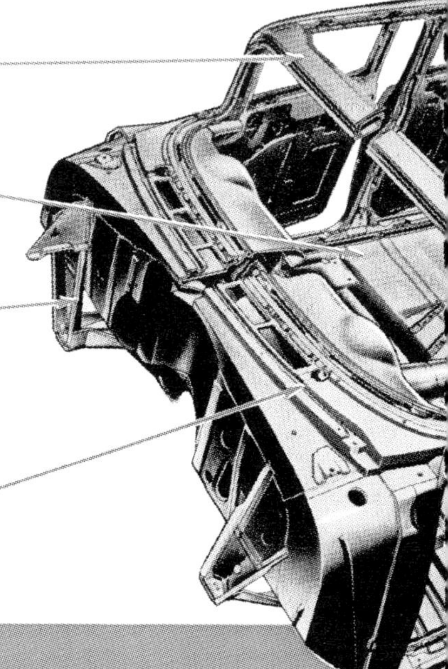

NEW BODY STRUCTURE

The new Fisher Unisteel body is a solid steel unit—with top, floor, cowl, deck frame, and sides fused into a single structure with double walls of steel.

A TOP THAT'S STRONG

The one-piece Turret Top is rigidly reinforced at its sides, ends, and across its middle to give the body maximum bracing from floor to roof and side to side. The narrow pillars that join the top to the base of the body are all rigid beams of reinforced box section.

A FLOOR THAT'S SOLID

The floor is made from heavy-gauge steel that's ribbed to make it stiffer, and is further strengthened by sills and cross beams, like basement beams in a house. In

this reinforcement, four U-channel cross beams are welded under the floor to form box sections between body sills that also form box sections with the floor.

NEW DOUBLE-WALLED COWL

Designed with double walls to form the plenum chamber for the unique new ventilation system, the cowl is actually two cowls—one within the other. Reinforced at its front and rear by the welded-in dash and instrument panels, it spans the frame, giving a firm arch-type support to the front of the body.

NEW DASH-TO-FRAME ATTACHMENT

Rigid braces help maintain accurate alignment of body and frame, and are scientifically located to reduce transmission of vibration and road shock to the passenger compartment.

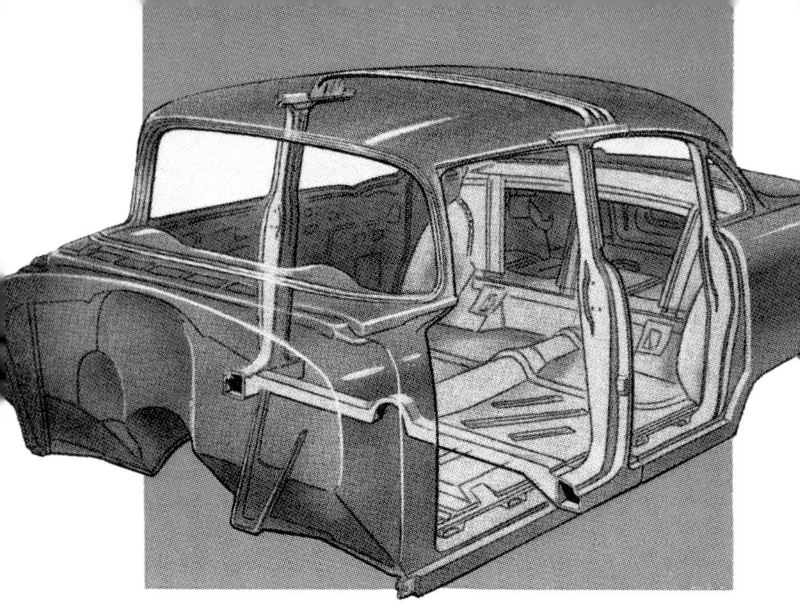

RIGID MID-BODY FRAME

A feature found in no other low-priced car is the rugged frame that girds the center of the body. Here Chevrolet's exclusive central roof bow and center pillars are strengthened by a floor cross beam and all are welded into a sturdy four-square structure.

NEW UNITIZED SIDES

Another body feature is "unitized side frame construction." From the cowl to the rear fender, each body side is precision-built as a unit, assuring accurate door fits. All doors and the rear quarters, including the integral rear fenders, are full-panelled box structures with double-walled strength.

SOLID REAR QUARTER BRACE

The rear structure is made strong by integral lateral bracing. The seat back support which merges into the parcel shelf; the shelf which merges into the

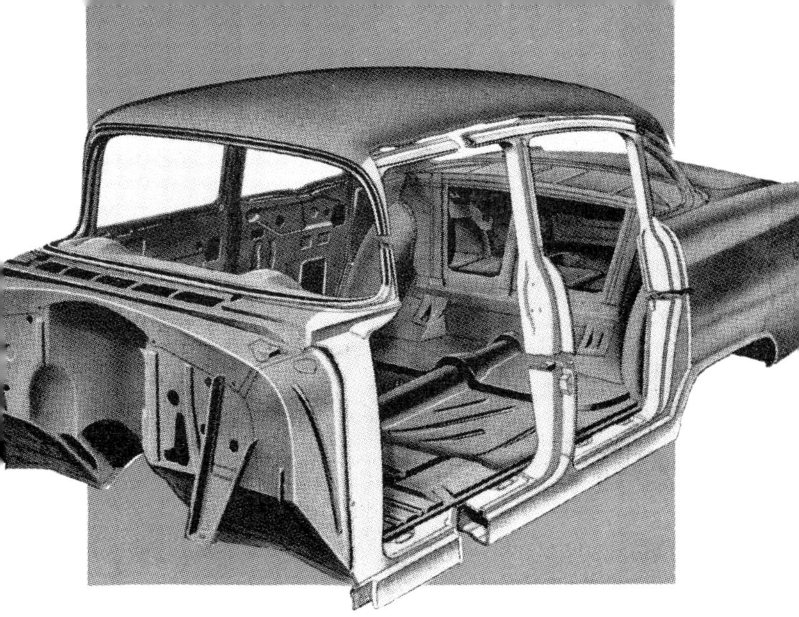

deck frame, which in turn merges into the lower end panel—all these are fused together to form a rigid box-like brace between the body sides. Further cross-strength is added by the gravel guard, which is now integral with the lower end panel. Integral wheel houses help to form a square-braced rear that is topped by the double-walled deck lid.

PRESERVED STRENGTH

To add years to their life, the complete body and the front sheet metal are finished in a nine-step process. The steps include alkaline cleaning and rust proofing, a primer coat, glaze coat, wet sanding, three coats of pyroxylin lacquer, a sound deadener application, and the machine polishing that gives the Chevrolet its lasting luster.

In addition, well-placed drainage holes in construction pockets throughout the car prevent water that might seep into the pockets from collecting and rusting through the enclosing metal.

Supported on a central rubber cushion at its front, the sheet metal structure rides steady in relation to the body, even on the roughest roads, without destructive and annoying weaving. The rigid fenders are solidly bolted to the cowl and connected by the wall of beams to which the radiator is mounted. Their inner walls serve as the sides of the engine compartment. The hood, now a single panel, is stiffened by flanges at its edges and cross beams at its ends. By means of new counterbalancing, with gear-type hinges, and a new latch and safety catch, it may be unlatched and lifted by one hand in an easy continuous motion, and closed and locked in a single movement. The hood opening is both lower and broader, and everything in the engine compartment that must be serviced is in easy reach.

RIDE . . . Features

QUADRA-POISE RIDE

- Balanced weight distribution.
- Long wheelbase; broad, nearly equal treads.
- Seats cradled between front and rear wheels.
- Low center of gravity.

GLIDE-RIDE FRONT SUSPENSION

- Inclined Knee-Action coil springs.
- Airplane-type shock absorbers mounted inside springs.
- Non-metallic-lined, spherical control-arm outer joints.
- Rubber-insulated control-arm inner pivots.
- Rubber control-arm bumpers.
- Unique braking dive control.
- Only four lubrication points.

OUTRIGGER REAR SUSPENSION

- Extra-long semi-elliptic springs.
- Outside-the-frame spring mountings.
- Rubber-insulation at both ends of springs.
- Compression-type shackles.
- Lubrication-eliminating spring leaf end liners.
- Diagonally-mounted airplane-type shock absorbers.
- Three rubber axle bumpers.

WIDE-BASE WHEELS AND TIRES

- Short-spoke steel disk wheels.
- Five-inch wide-base wheel rims.
- Extra-low-pressure tubeless tires.

A COMPLETELY NEW DRIVING AND RIDING SENSATION!

Like riding on a cloud! No question about it—the Motoramic Chevrolet is engineered for wonderfully new driving and riding comfort . . . softer, smoother, and safer than ever before.

NEW QUADRA-POISE RIDE

From the new Glide-Ride Front Suspension to the location and construction of seats . . . from the softer-riding tubeless tires to the new Outrigger Rear Suspension, new designs and features have been incorporated in the Motoramic Chevrolet to assure better riding comfort, better roadability, and even greater stability.

Its lower center of gravity, well-distributed weight, and wider tread (actually the same as the standard railroad gauge!) combine to give a safer, road-hugging ride. Both front and rear treads measure nearly the same—this means easier tracking on rutted country roads. The Motoramic Chevrolet is built closer to the ground, yet there's more room inside. Seats are cradled between front and rear wheels—positioned for maximum riding comfort.

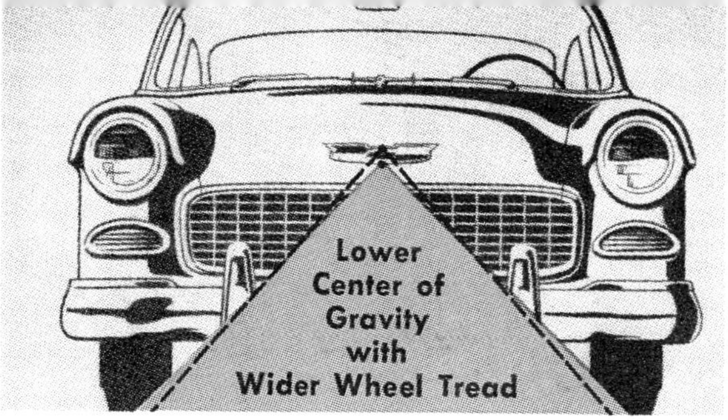

With the new front suspension, large coil springs and new spherical joint steering knuckles flex freely —each wheel independent of the other—to level road bumps. Here is a completely new and unique design that makes Chevrolet's famed Knee-Action more gentle than ever. Double-acting shock absorbers not only cushion spring action, but stabilize sway and body roll. The new rubber engine- and body-mounts, and new pedal and steering gear mountings, further isolate vibrations and road shocks from the driver and passengers.

The new rear springs are both longer and wider, and they're attached to the *outside* of the frame . . . spaced wider apart to give greater stability in cornering. And adding the final touch to Chevrolet's satin-smooth ride—the new Hotchkiss Drive cushions drive-line shocks through the rear springs. As an extra, exclusive feature, Chevrolet's new Braking Dive Control assures "heads up" stops whenever the brakes are applied.

NEW COMPRESSION-TYPE
REAR SPRING SHACKLES
NEW EXTRA-LONG REAR SPRINGS,
WITH RUBBER-INSULATED ENDS
NEW RUBBER AXLE BUMPERS
NEW OUTRIGGER REAR SPRING MOUNTINGS
NEW HOTCHKISS DRIVE

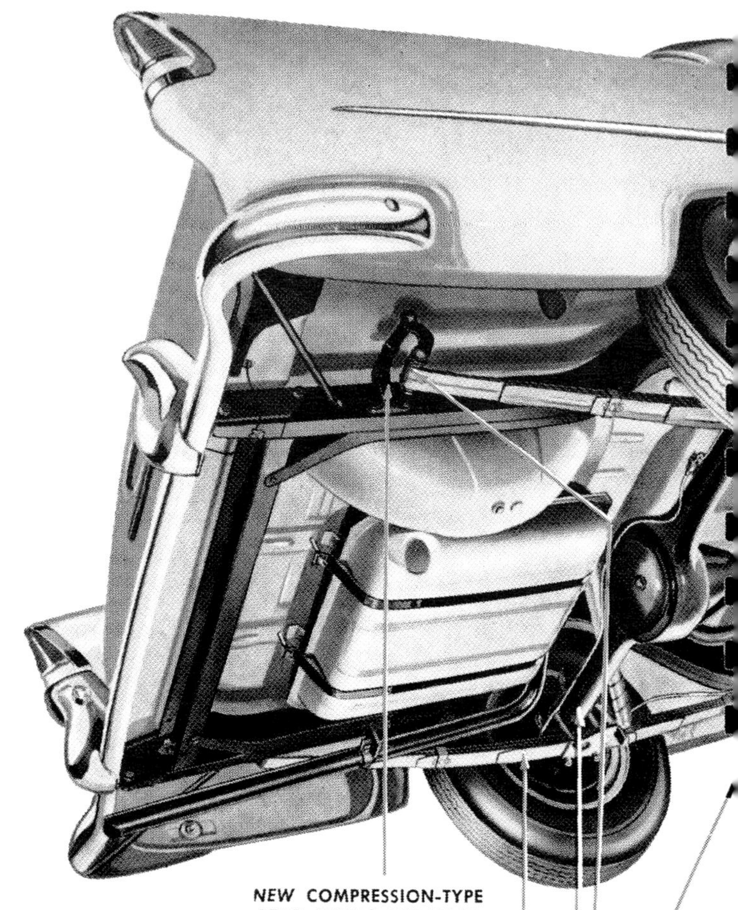

Ride

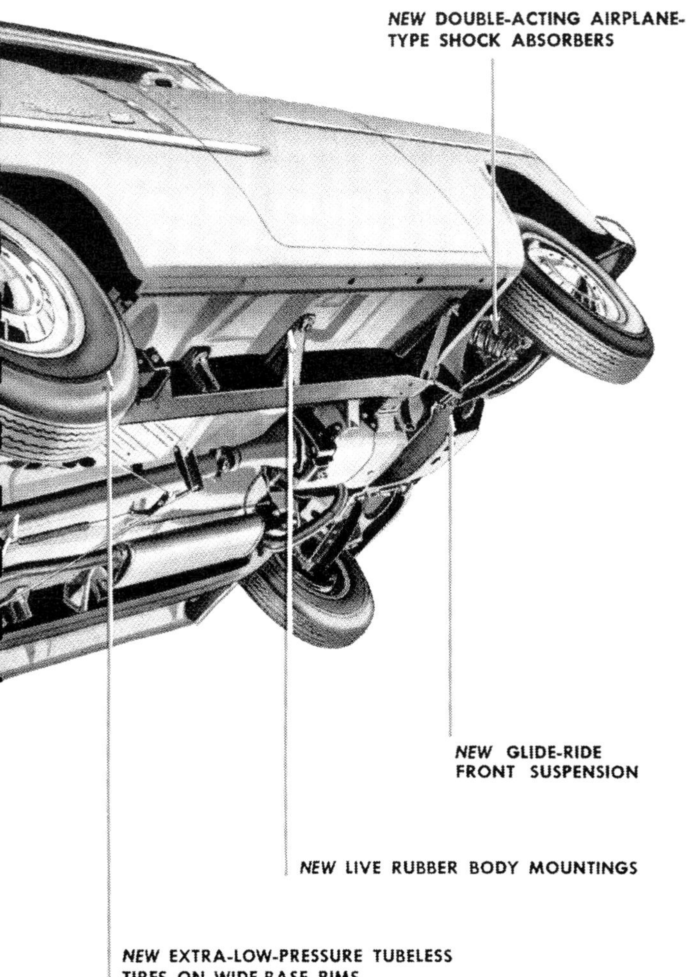

ONLY *FOUR* LUBRICATION POINTS . . . IN THE WHOLE RIDING SYSTEM!

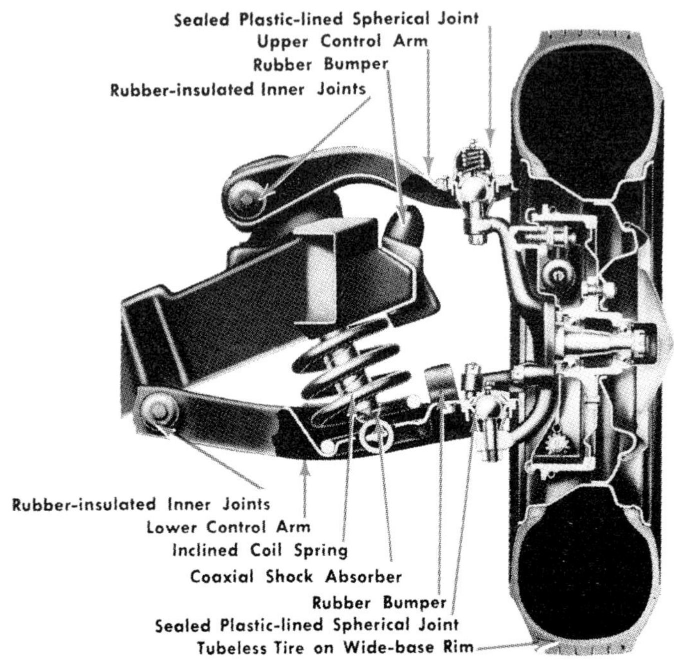

NEW GLIDE-RIDE FRONT SUSPENSION

With its completely new design, Chevrolet's famed Knee-Action is smoother than ever. Stability is improved through the 1.3-inch wider tread and lower center of gravity. In fact, because of the increased stability, a stabilizer bar is no longer necessary.

UNIQUE NEW SPHERICAL-JOINT SUSPENSION

Sealed, self-adjusting, spherical-joint steering knuckles are housed in the outer ends of the pan-shaped control arms . . . are lined with an exceptionally long-wearing new plastic material. Rubber insulation, in the inner joints of the arms, reduces the transmission of shock and vibration; rubber bumpers absorb the severest jolts. Because of the new joints, only four lubrication points are needed for the entire system.

Ride

NEW TILTED COIL SPRINGS

Made of tough chrome alloy steel, the front springs
are mounted with the upper ends inclined inward.
This provides greater operating efficiency, increases
stability, and minimizes spring distortion.

LIFE-SEALED TUBULAR SHOCK ABSORBERS

Direct double-acting shock absorbers are mounted
within the springs. Permanently lubricated, they
have a large fluid capacity, accurate valve action,
and provide excellent ride control in any climate.

NEW TUBELESS TIRES

Extra-low-pressure tubeless tires are provided on
all Motoramic Chevrolets. Their features include
greater resistance to blowouts and slower deflation
if punctured. This is due to the integral butyl liner
which clings to any sharp object that penetrates the
tire. In addition, they make car handling easier and
riding softer. In construction, tubeless tires are
similar to conventional casings. The conventional
wheel valve hole is retained and a snap-in rubber
valve replaces the inner tube valve stem. Tubeless
tires with white side walls are optional.

SHORT-SPOKE STEEL WHEELS

Chevrolet's wide-base wheel rims allow straighter
tire side walls; provide a better support to prevent
side roll. The four openings that form the spokes
in the wheel, make possible the use of strap-on
chains.

NEW BRAKING DIVE CONTROL

Made possible by the new suspension geometry, this
exclusive feature reduces braking dive up to 45 per
cent, lessening the danger of front-end damage or
locked bumpers in tight-traffic driving.

The new rear springs are mounted outside the frame side rails instead of below them as in other low-priced cars, placing the springs farther apart for greater riding stability. Moreover, they are the longest in Chevrolet's field, to make riding smoother.

The springs are made up of four leaves (five, in station wagons) of chrome alloy steel, and the main leaf is shot-peened for greater resistance to flexing fatigue. Six-leaf heavy-duty springs are available. Spring leaf end liners eliminate the need for lubrication. Rubber insulates the mounting of the springs in their front hangers and rear shackles. Compression type shackles provide unhampered spring action.

Direct-acting shock absorbers, like those in front, control "bottoming" and "pitching" motion. Diagonal mounting utilizes a longer piston travel; provides greater resistance to sway.

NEW HOTCHKISS DRIVE

With Chevrolet's new Hotchkiss drive system, the rear axle and wheels are connected to the chassis frame solely through the rear springs. As a result, drive-line shocks are cushioned by the springs. Three rubber bumpers, two on the axle housing and one above its center, snub severe impacts.

ENGINES . . . Features

CHOICE OF THREE GREAT ENGINES
- World's most advanced valve-in-head V8.
- *Two* modern valve-in-head sixes.
- Four high horsepower ratings.

HIGH-COMPRESSION PERFORMANCE
- High turbulence combustion chambers.
- High power-to-weight ratio.

PROVED VALVE-IN-HEAD DESIGN
- Highly efficient breathing.
- Rugged valve operating mechanism.
- Hydraulic valve lifters (Powerglide).

ADVANCED CARBURETION SYSTEM
- Concentric bowl carburetor (Sixes).
- Balanced-flow dual carburetor (V8).
- High performance 4-barrel carburetor (V8 option).

ALL-WEATHER IGNITION SYSTEM
- Dual automatic spark control.
- Tight-sealing terminal connections.
- Non-metallic high tension cables.

HIGH-EFFICIENCY 12-VOLT ELECTRICAL SYSTEM
- High-capacity generator.
- High-speed positive-shift starter.

CONTROLLED FULL-PRESSURE LUBRICATION
- Scientific oil distribution.
- Floating oil pump intake.

ADVANCED POWER-HUSHED COOLING
- Quiet, slow-turning fan.
- High-volume coolant pump.
- Full-length cylinder cooling.

POISED-POWER ENGINE MOUNTINGS
- Dynamically balanced four-point system.

POWER, WHEN NEEDED . . . FOR SAFETY!

POWER

... for every need or desire!

The Motoramic Chevrolet presents the widest choice of power ever offered in a low-priced car . . . three great new valve-in-head engines—V8 or six—with four power ratings . . . power for every need or desire!

To those who want an overhead valve V8, Chevrolet presents the new "Turbo-Fire V8"—the newest, most advanced power plant in the industry! To those who prefer a six, Chevrolet offers the choice of two of the finest valve-in-head sixes ever designed.

Each of these three great new engines is alive with power—high-compression power that means brilliant acceleration, swift, safer passing, and effortless cruising on hills or level highway. Each combines outstanding performance with entirely new fuel economy, and traditional Chevrolet durability that puts more miles of motoring pleasure in every dollar. For these fine new engines are the result of more than forty years of valve-in-head design leadership by Chevrolet—builder of more valve-in-head engines than all other manufacturers combined!

THREE GREAT NEW VALVE-IN-HEAD ENGINES

. . . with high-compression power!

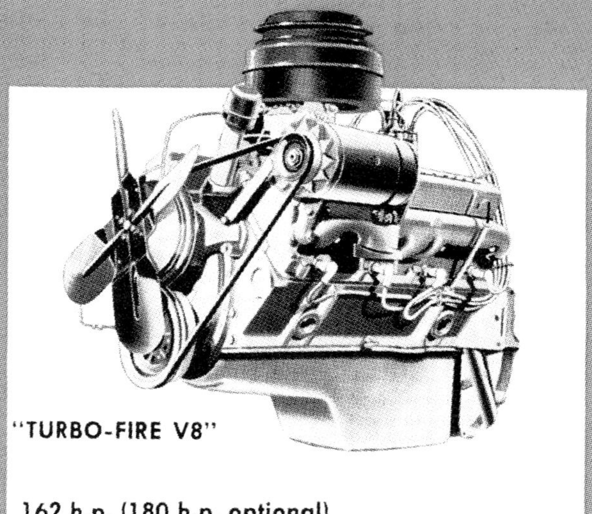

"TURBO-FIRE V8"

162 h.p. (180 h.p. optional)

136 h.p.

123 h.p.

TWO "BLUE-FLAME" SIXES

The NEW "TURBO-FIRE V8"

Chevrolet's new "Turbo-Fire V8" is far more than a new engine—it's a milestone in automotive history! Its design represents the highest degree of automotive engine development. Its high power with low weight provides spectacular performance. Its high mechanical efficiency results in exceptional economy and durability. And for smooth, quiet operation, it's unsurpassed.

NEW HIGHS IN PERFORMANCE AND ECONOMY

The highly efficient performance is the product of several design principles. Famous Chevrolet valve-in-head design permits a powerful volume of fuel mixture to be drawn into each cylinder with every intake stroke. New Fire-Swirl combustion chambers, with 8.0 to 1 compression, extract more power from every drop of fuel. A piston stroke of only three inches transmits more power to the crankshaft with less friction and heat loss. Low-resistance exhaust passages allow the engine to "breathe" more freely at any speed.

A NEW HIGH IN SMOOTHNESS

Many other features contribute to the pleasingly smooth and powerful feel of the "Turbo-Fire V8." Balanced carburetion, with a positive-action automatic choke, distributes a more uniform fuel mixture to each cylinder, regardless of climatic conditions. Large valves, with individual operating mechanisms, work smoothly and quietly. Hydraulic lifters (with Powerglide) eliminate periodic valve adjustment. Lightweight aluminum pistons and short, stiff connecting rods reduce bearing loads.

A NEW HIGH IN DURABILITY

The rigid, compact cylinder block keeps moving parts in perfect alignment. Five bearings support the precision-machined forged-steel crankshaft; five others support the long-wearing cast-alloy-iron camshaft. A multiple-link camshaft drive chain maintains split-second timing of valves and ignition.

A NEW HIGH IN BALANCE

An exceptionally high degree of balance is built into every "Turbo-Fire V8." During assembly, individual parts are carefully weight-matched and balanced to exacting standards. Then, each completed engine is placed in motion and balanced to perfection by a giant new machine developed especially for this operation. The final result is a smoother, quieter, finer-performing engine—an engine that establishes new standards of excellence in every detail!

STAR FEATURES OF
A STAR PERFORMER!

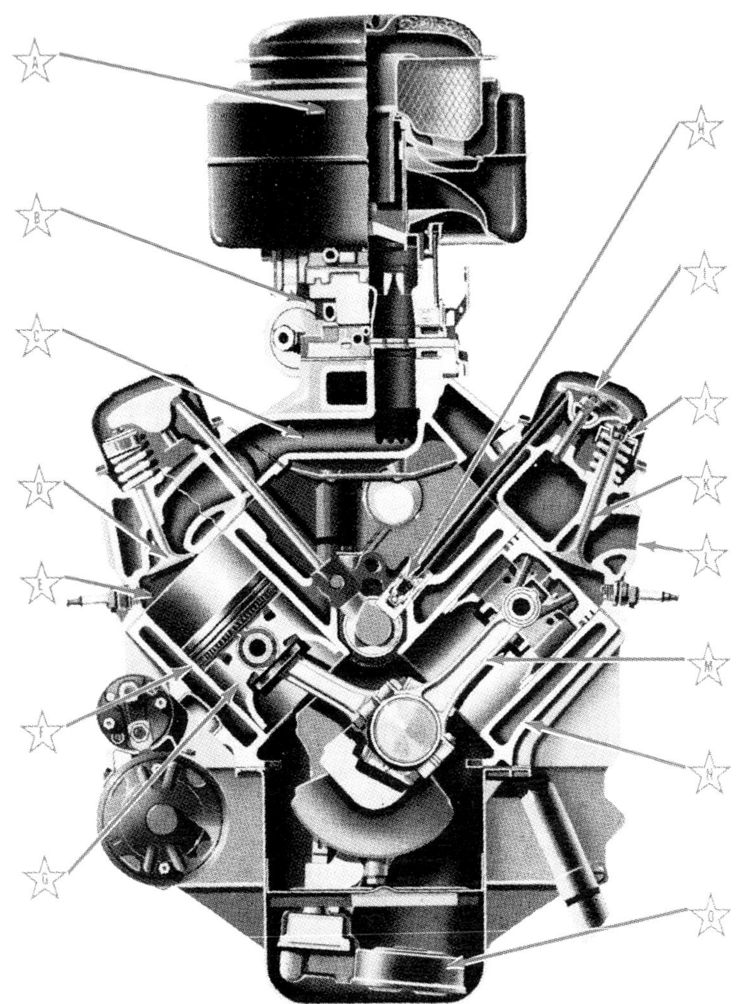

NEW "TURBO-FIRE V8" ENGINE

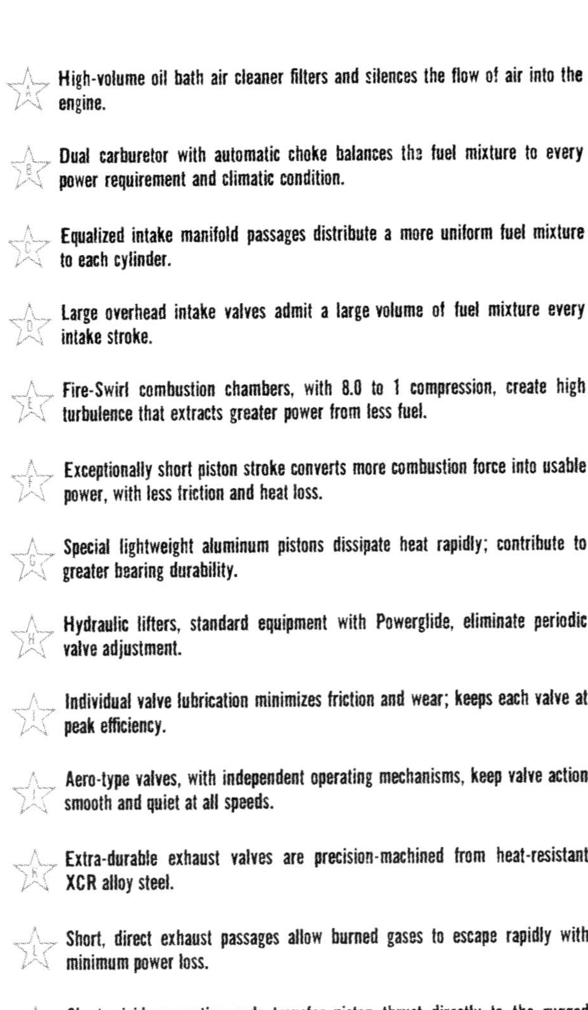

High-volume oil bath air cleaner filters and silences the flow of air into the engine.

Dual carburetor with automatic choke balances the fuel mixture to every power requirement and climatic condition.

Equalized intake manifold passages distribute a more uniform fuel mixture to each cylinder.

Large overhead intake valves admit a large volume of fuel mixture every intake stroke.

Fire-Swirl combustion chambers, with 8.0 to 1 compression, create high turbulence that extracts greater power from less fuel.

Exceptionally short piston stroke converts more combustion force into usable power, with less friction and heat loss.

Special lightweight aluminum pistons dissipate heat rapidly; contribute to greater bearing durability.

Hydraulic lifters, standard equipment with Powerglide, eliminate periodic valve adjustment.

Individual valve lubrication minimizes friction and wear; keeps each valve at peak efficiency.

Aero-type valves, with independent operating mechanisms, keep valve action smooth and quiet at all speeds.

Extra-durable exhaust valves are precision-machined from heat-resistant XCR alloy steel.

Short, direct exhaust passages allow burned gases to escape rapidly with minimum power loss.

Short, rigid connecting rods transfer piston thrust directly to the rugged precision-balanced crankshaft.

Generous coolant areas maintain proper operating temperatures throughout the engine.

Controlled full-pressure lubrication, with floating intake, extends the life of every moving part.

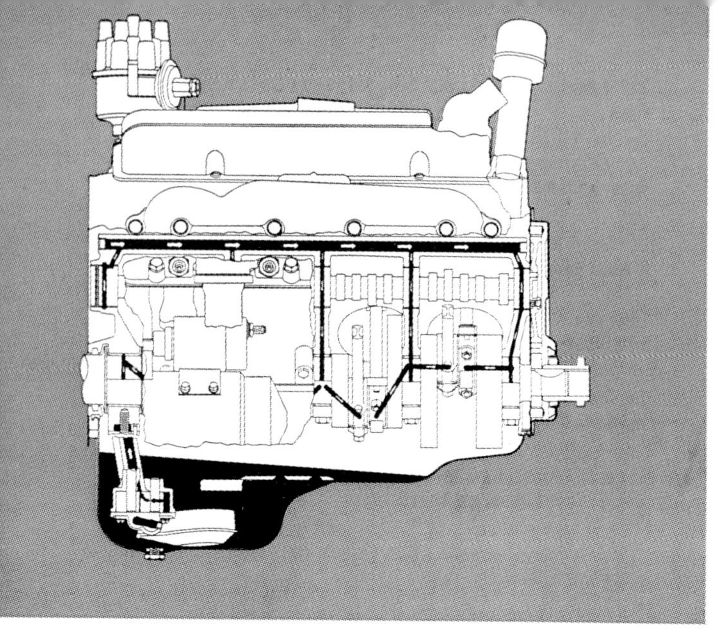

CONTROLLED FULL-PRESSURE LUBRICATION

An important factor in the efficient operation and outstanding durability of the "Turbo-Fire V8" is its controlled full-pressure lubrication system. Every moving part is supplied with the right quantity of oil at precisely the right time, under the most effective pressure. And this highly efficient system actually requires less oil—the refill capacity of just four quarts means extra savings with every oil change. The floating oil pump intake picks up only the cleanest oil, which is temperature-conditioned by integral passages in the block. The main oil gallery between the cylinder banks is supplied directly from the pump, and distributes the flow of pressurized oil throughout the engine. Two parallel galleries provide positive, metered oil feed to each valve mechanism. Pressurized oil is conveyed through the drilled crankshaft to each connecting rod bearing and cylinder wall. Effective crankcase ventilation removes harmful vapors, and keeps the lubricating oil fresh longer.

Here's an optional "Turbo-Fire V8" engine that develops a full 180 horsepower—smooth, quiet responsive power that gives the Motoramic Chevrolet performance never before possible in any low-priced car. This great new engine includes all the advanced basic Chevrolet V8 design features, *plus:*

- High-performance four-barrel carburetor
- Special matching intake manifold
- Heavy-duty oil bath air cleaner
- Free-flow dual exhaust system

TWO GREAT NEW SIXES!

"Blue-Flame 136"

.. engineered and built specifically for automatic driving with Powerglide.

"Blue-Flame 123"

. . . developed for thriftiest driving with standard or overdrive transmissions

Engines

UNMATCHED POWER CHOICE

With *two* great new valve-in-head sixes, the Motoramic Chevrolet presents a power choice that is unmatched in the low-price field. Each of these engines combines the latest engineering advances with design principles that have been proved by more than forty years of Chevrolet valve-in-head leadership. And in these two new "Blue-Flame" engines, Chevrolet presents the valve-in-head six at its best . . . the most thoroughly proved and most *popular* six-cylinder automotive engine design.

MOST POPULAR DESIGN

There are many reasons for the outstanding popularity enjoyed by the valve-in-head six. From a design standpoint, it is relatively simple, inherently smooth-running, and highly efficient. These benefits also contribute in large measure to its rugged dependability and exceptional economy of operation.

When Chevrolet introduced the valve-in-head six to the low-price field, it was a well-established power plant of medium-priced cars. Since then, the valve-in-head design has been adopted by more and more manufacturers, and is now offered in nearly every price class, including many of the world's finest, most costly cars. So great has been the public acceptance of the Chevrolet design that Chevrolet has produced more valve-in-head engines than all other manufacturers combined!

IMPORTANT DESIGN FEATURES

While the "Blue-Flame 136" and "Blue-Flame 123" are individually engineered to the specific requirements of their particular power teams, many important basic design features are common to both. Some of these features are shown on the next page in a cross-section of the new "Blue-Flame 136."

FAMOUS FEATURES OF CHEVROLET'S FAMOUS SIXES

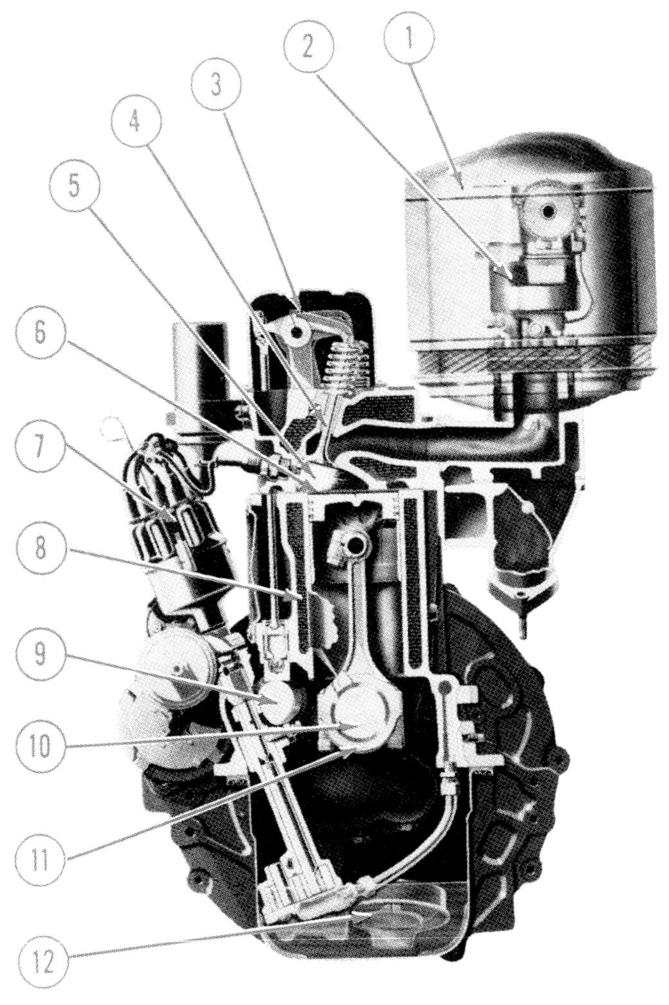

"BLUE-FLAME 136" ILLUSTRATED

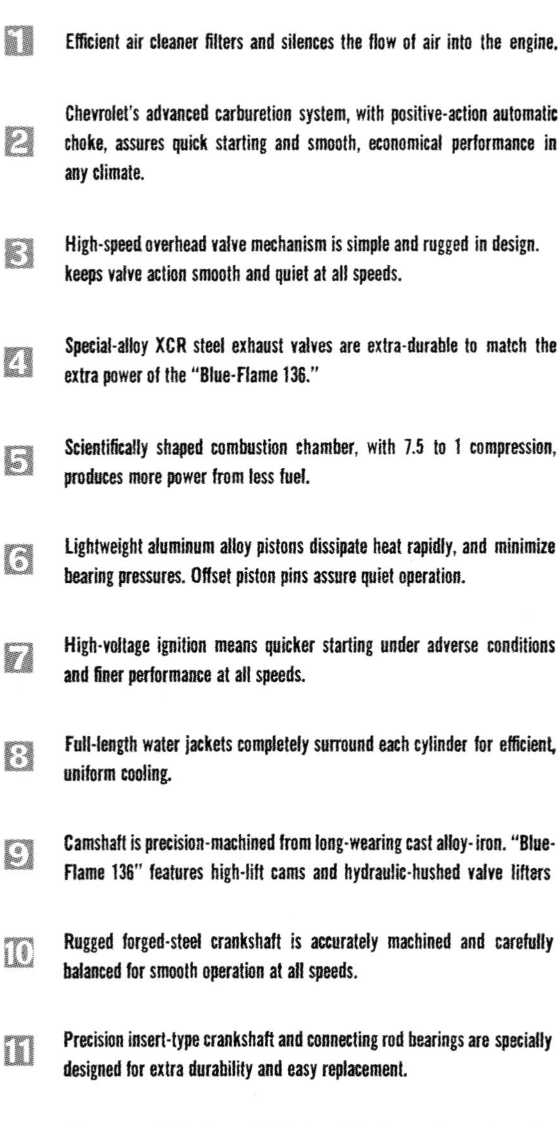

1 Efficient air cleaner filters and silences the flow of air into the engine.

2 Chevrolet's advanced carburetion system, with positive-action automatic choke, assures quick starting and smooth, economical performance in any climate.

3 High-speed overhead valve mechanism is simple and rugged in design. keeps valve action smooth and quiet at all speeds.

4 Special-alloy XCR steel exhaust valves are extra-durable to match the extra power of the "Blue-Flame 136."

5 Scientifically shaped combustion chamber, with 7.5 to 1 compression, produces more power from less fuel.

6 Lightweight aluminum alloy pistons dissipate heat rapidly, and minimize bearing pressures. Offset piston pins assure quiet operation.

7 High-voltage ignition means quicker starting under adverse conditions and finer performance at all speeds.

8 Full-length water jackets completely surround each cylinder for efficient, uniform cooling.

9 Camshaft is precision-machined from long-wearing cast alloy-iron. "Blue-Flame 136" features high-lift cams and hydraulic-hushed valve lifters

10 Rugged forged-steel crankshaft is accurately machined and carefully balanced for smooth operation at all speeds.

11 Precision insert-type crankshaft and connecting rod bearings are specially designed for extra durability and easy replacement.

12 Full-pressure lubrication, with floating oil intake, supplies each moving part with effective, controlled lubrication at all engine speeds.

BASIC DESIGN ADVANTAGES
of the Chevrolet Sixes

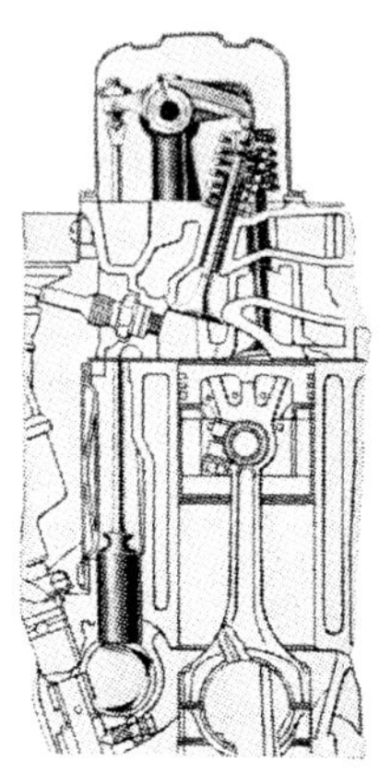

HIGH-COMPRESSION VALVE-IN-HEAD DESIGN

Proved valve-in-head design is the basis of Chevrolet's outstanding power and economy. Large valves admit a powerful fuel charge with every intake stroke. The high 7.5 to 1 compression squeezes more power from every drop of fuel. And Chevrolet's scientifically-shaped combustion chamber converts more explosive force into usable power.

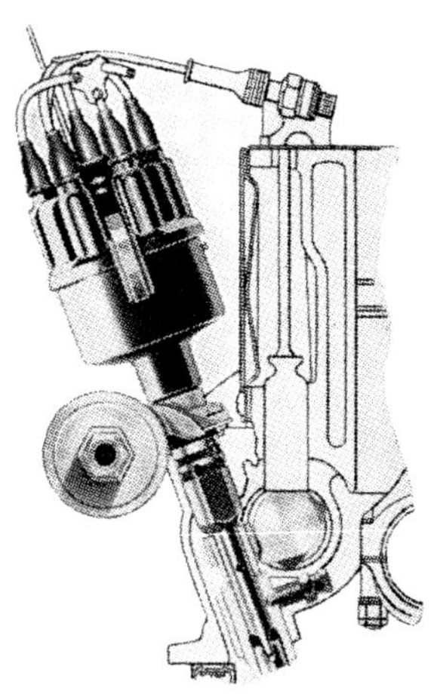

NEW HIGH-VOLTAGE IGNITION

Chevrolet's new high-voltage ignition means greater ignition dependability, better starting, and more efficient battery charging. The new high-tower distributor features precision spark control with both vacuum and centrifugal advance. The unified oil pump drive stabilizes the distributor shaft rotation—improves breaker point action and assures a hotter, more concentrated spark.

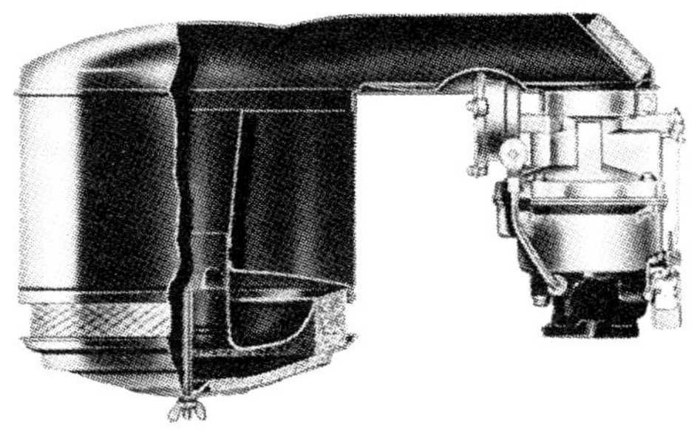

Chevrolet's advanced carburetion system is engineered for smooth performance and efficient, economical operation. The new low-mount air cleaner filters and silences the flow of air into the carburetor, and the positive-action automatic choke assures quick, convenient starting and smooth warmup in any climate. The concentric carburetor has twin floats that maintain a balanced fuel mixture even on curves or grades.

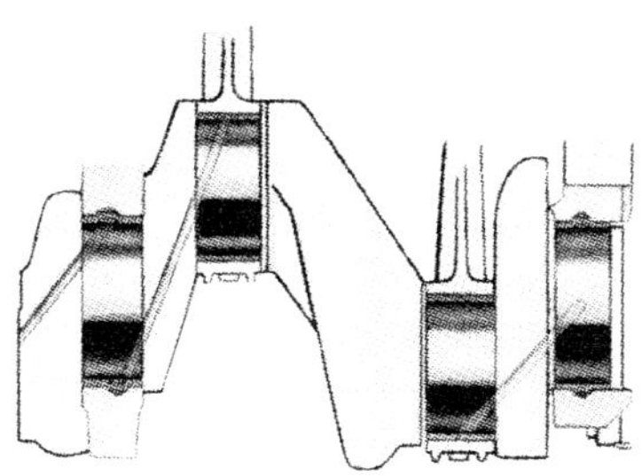

Chevrolet's forged steel crankshaft is engineered and built for extra strength and durability. Its bearing surfaces are precision machined to close tolerances. Then the entire crankshaft is carefully balanced to exacting standards. Crankshaft main and connecting rod journals are fitted with replaceable precision bearings, made of specially selected alloys.

Chevrolet's full-pressure lubrication system maintains controlled, effective lubrication at all speeds, and assures efficient performance and maximum durability. The new floating oil intake picks up only the cleanest oil, which is forced under pressure into the main oil gallery extending along one side of the crankcase. From here, pressurized oil is distributed through each main bearing to the camshaft bearings, and to the connecting rods and cylinder walls through drilled passages in the crankshaft. Oil from the camshaft rear bearing supplies the valve lifter gallery, and is then metered to the overhead valve system. Positive timing gear lubrication is assured by a small jet which allows pressurized oil to flow over the revolving gears.

FEATURES FOUND IN ALL 1955 CHEVROLET ENGINES

HARMONIC BALANCER

A feature of the world's finest engines, the crank-shaft-mounted vibration damper absorbs minor power-impulses—keeps the flow of power smoother and quieter.

FINER FUEL SYSTEM

A new pulsator-type fuel pump maintains a smoother, more constant flow of fuel to the carburetor. No periodic cleaning is required, because the entire fuel system is protected by a special filter, in the gasoline tank, that screens out harmful dirt particles and prevents water from entering the fuel line where it might freeze. Its large area makes it practically clog-proof.

NEW POWER-HUSHED COOLING

Because Chevrolet valve-in-head engines are highly efficient, more combustion force is converted into usable power, and less heat is lost to the cooling system. In any climate, the engine quickly attains and maintains the proper operating temperature. Controlled circulation maintains proper temperatures throughout the engine, assuring maximum power, economy, and durability.

In addition to these proved design features, Chevrolet's new Power-Hushed cooling introduces important new advances. The new large-diameter fan maintains high air flow at all engine speeds yet revolves more slowly to keep fan roar at a minimum. The new high-capacity by-pass type water pump maintains proper coolant circulation at lower speeds. The new low, wide free-flow radiator dissipates heat rapidly. And the pressure type radiator cap increases cooling capacity under extreme conditions.

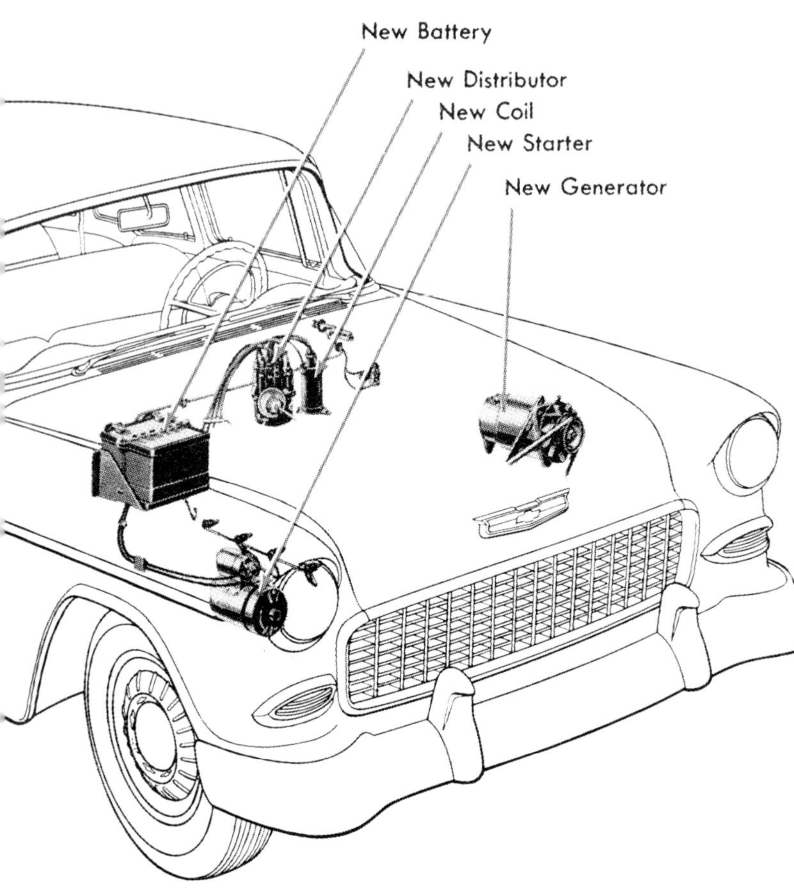

NEW HIGH-EFFICIENCY
12-VOLT ELECTRICAL SYSTEM

Just recently, improved electrical systems were adopted by several of America's higher-priced cars. Now, the Motoramic Chevrolet introduces the high-efficiency 12-volt electrical system to the low-price field . . . and adds still another laurel to an already impressive list of famous Chevrolet "firsts."

Chevrolet's new 12-volt electrical system offers many important advantages. Superior ignition means a hotter spark, quicker starting under adverse conditions, and more reliable firing—particularly at higher engine speeds. Greater generator efficiency results in a faster-cranking starter, less chance of a rundown battery, and extra power to operate the lights, radio, heater fan, and all the modern power features available with the Motoramic Chevrolet.

SUPERIOR IGNITION

New super-efficient ignition permits quicker starting in any weather and finer over-all engine performance. A special wiring circuit enables the weatherproof 12-volt coil to develop an extra-powerful spark for starting. The new high-tower distributor improves the insulation of the ignition system and automatically maintains a precisely timed spark under all operating conditions. Non-metallic high-tension cables with moisture-proof caps deliver higher voltage to the heavy-duty spark plugs. The result is a hotter spark, more reliable ignition, longer spark plug life, and a smoother-running engine.

GREATER ELECTRICAL POWER

With 12 volts, Chevrolet's entire electrical system is more efficient—with greater power reserve for lighting and operation of all electrical equipment. The new 54-plate battery provides a full 12 volts . . . has extra capacity for extra-heavy-duty operation. The new high-efficiency generator produces a full 25 amperes at 12 volts (the equivalent of 50 amperes at 6 volts) to maintain high battery charge under all driving conditions. And Chevrolet's famous positive-shift starter is now finer than ever—extra power and faster cranking mean quick, sure starting in any weather.

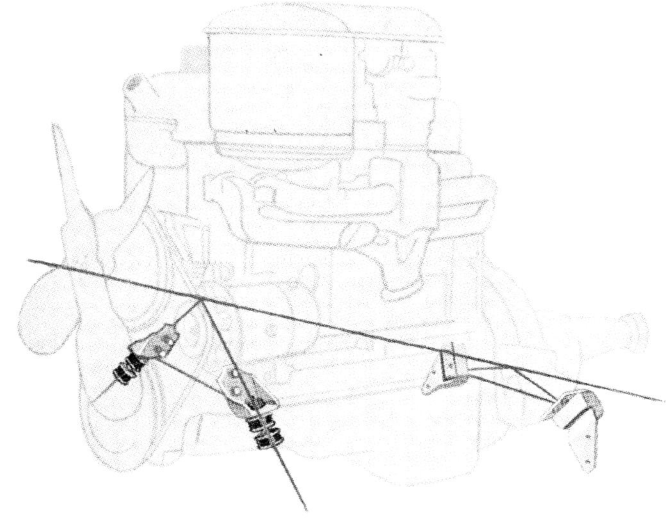

Chevrolet's new Poised-Power engine mountings isolate engine movements and vibration from the frame and body. Four large rubber mountings are located at strategic balance points, at scientifically engineered mounting angles. The entire power plant is poised in balance, and annoying vibrations are smothered before they can be transmitted to the rest of the car.

NEW FREEDOM FROM VIBRATION

In addition to the isolation from engine vibrations that is provided by the Poised-Power engine mountings, special care is taken to prevent the transmission of road shocks and engine vibrations to the driving controls through their linkages to the engine or chassis. As the result, the driver of a Motoramic Chevrolet experiences a freedom from annoying sensations in his controls such as is experienced in few other cars.

CHOICE OF SIX GREAT POWER TEAMS
- "Turbo-Fire V8" with Powerglide, Overdrive, or Synchro-Mesh Transmission.
- "Blue-Flame" Sixes with Powerglide, Overdrive, or Synchro-Mesh Transmission.

TIP-TOE-MAGIC CLUTCH
- Heavy-duty friction disk.
- Extra-easy diaphragm spring actuation.
- Permanently lubricated ball release bearing.

HEAVY-DUTY QUIET-EASE SYNCHRO-MESH TRANSMISSION
- Synchro-mesh second- and third-speed gears.
- Extra-quiet, hardened, shot-peened helical gears.

OPTIONAL, ECONOMICAL, TOUCH-DOWN OVERDRIVE TRANSMISSION
- Three-pinion planetary gear overdrive.
- Electric engagement controlled through accelerator.
- Manual overdrive lockout.

OPTIONAL SUPER-SMOOTH POWER-GLIDE AUTOMATIC TRANSMISSION
- Three-element hydraulic torque converter.
- Controlled oil cooling.
- Constant-mesh helical planetary gears.
- Positive parking lock.
- Safety switch in starter circuit.

HOTCHKISS DRIVE
- Tubular propeller shaft.
- Needle-bearing universal joints.

SEMI-FLOATING REAR AXLE
- Quiet and durable hypoid drive gears.
- Two-pinion differential.
- Large flanged axle shafts.
- Single-unit banjo-type housing.

***THE BIGGEST POWER-DRIVE
CHOICE IN CHEVROLET HISTORY!***

POWER DRIVE...

velvet smooth transmission

of engine power to the wheels

The Motoramic Chevrolet offers the biggest power-drive selection in Chevrolet history—to provide just the right combination of driving convenience, car performance, and operating economy for everyone.

SIX NEW POWER TEAMS

Smoother, quieter, and more dependable than ever. That's the best description of Chevrolet's new flow of power from the engine to the wheels, through any of Chevrolet's three new drive trains. To better transmit the power of the new engines, all units in each drive train—transmission, propeller shaft, universal joints, and rear axle—are new or redesigned. All were engineered to work as a team. And each power team was completely road tested for extremes in operation, performance, and durability—far beyond any tests it would receive under normal consumer use—before being O.K.'d. The only question the prospect need answer is, "What combination of convenience, performance, and economy do I prefer?"

"TURBO-FIRE V8"
Powerglide—Economiser Axle

All the convenience of completely automatic driving at its best . . . with brilliant acceleration, effortless cruising, and outstanding economy of operation. 162 horsepower (or 180 with Super "Turbo-Fire V8"). 3.55 to 1 axle ratio.

"BLUE-FLAME 136"
Powerglide—Economiser Axle

Wonderful performance with automatic driving at lowest cost. 136 horsepower. 3.55 to 1 axle ratio.

"TURBO-FIRE V8"
Overdrive—Power-Master Axle

A marvelous combination of power, economy, and simplified driving. 162 horsepower (or 180 with Super "Turbo-Fire V8"). 4.11 to 1 axle ratio.

"BLUE-FLAME 123"
Overdrive—Power-Master Axle

Fine performance with maximum fuel savings and minimum upkeep. 123 horsepower. 4.11 to 1 axle ratio.

"TURBO-FIRE V8"
Synchro-Mesh—Fuel-Saver Axle

Manual gearshifting with the maximum in low-cost power. 162 horsepower (or 180 with Super "Turbo-Fire V8"). 3.7 to 1 axle ratio.

"BLUE-FLAME 123"
Synchro-Mesh—Fuel-Saver Axle

Power in its most economical form. 123 horsepower. 3.7 to 1 axle ratio.

NEW COMPONENTS OF THE SIX NEW POWER TEAMS

NEW ENGINES	NEW CLUTCHES
New 162- or 180-hp "Turbo-Fire V8"	No clutch
New 136-hp "Blue-Flame" Six	
New 162- or 180-hp "Turbo-Fire V8"	New 10" diameter Tip-Toe-Magic Clutch
New 123-hp "Blue-Flame" Six	New 9 ½" diameter Tip-Toe-Magic Clutch
New 162- or 180-hp "Turbo-Fire V8"	New 10" diameter Tip-Toe-Magic Clutch
New 123-hp "Blue-Flame" Six	New 9 ½" diameter Tip-Toe-Magic Clutch

NEW TRANSMISSIONS	NEW DRIVE SYSTEM	NEW REAR AXLES
Improved Powerglide Automatic Transmission		New 3.55 to 1 Economiser axle
New Touch-Down Overdrive Transmission;	New Hotchkiss propeller shaft and universal joints	New 4.11 to 1 Power-Master axle
New Synchro-Mesh Transmission		New 3.7 to 1 Fuel-Saver axle

Chevrolet clutches are the single dry plate type but feature a superior method of operation. Instead of having many coil springs and pressure levers to engage the clutch disk, a single dish-like diaphragm spring with integral fingers pointing inward is used. When moved by the clutch release lever, the fingers flex forward to disengage the clutch and, when released, flex back to engage it—with an action similar to the flexing action of the bottom of an oil can. When they are released, the rim of the diaphragm spring engages the pressure plate with a uniform pressure so that it makes full uniform contact with the clutch disk. Because of the diaphragm spring, clutch operation is smoother but firmer, and less pedal pressure is required. For 1955, the clutch disks are enlarged to 9½ inches diameter with the six-cylinder engines and ten inches with the V8. Then, too, a new clutch linkage eliminates transfer of engine vibrations to the driver's foot.

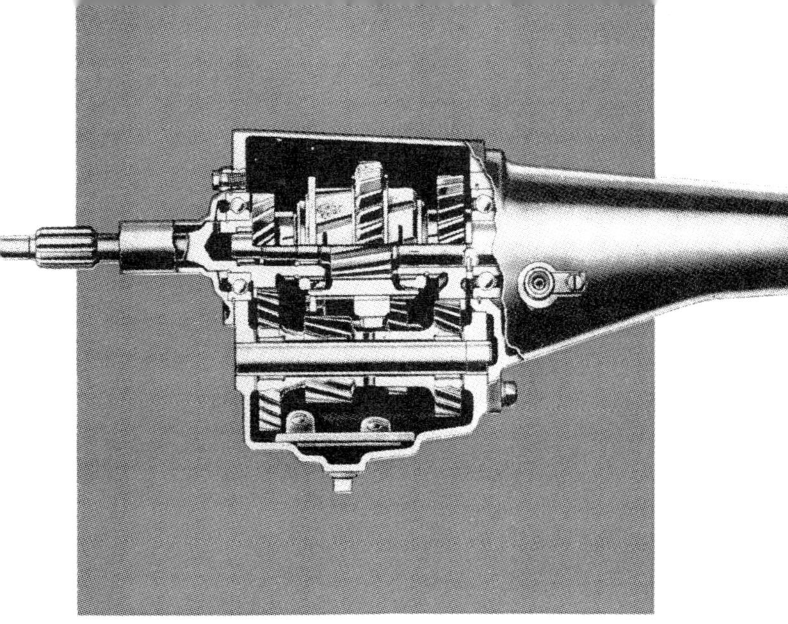

MORE DURABLE SYNCHRO-MESH TRANSMISSION

Chevrolet's famous manual gearshift transmission is called "Synchro-Mesh" because, before a shift into second or third is made, the speeds of the gears are synchronized. In this way, the gears are aligned so that when the shift is made, it is done quietly, with ease and smoothness—even by the least experienced driver. All the gears have durable, silently meshing helical teeth and nearly every bearing is of the freely turning ball or roller type. To handle the great power of the new 1955 engines, this famous transmission has been completely redesigned for even greater torque transmitting ability and even greater durability. The mainshaft and its rear support bearing are larger. All gears are now shot-peened after hardening, for longer wear. The ends of the gear teeth are rounded instead of angle-shaped — this means even smoother shifting and longer-lasting teeth. And a baffle in the bottom of the transmission housing traps metal fragments that might damage the gears and bearings.

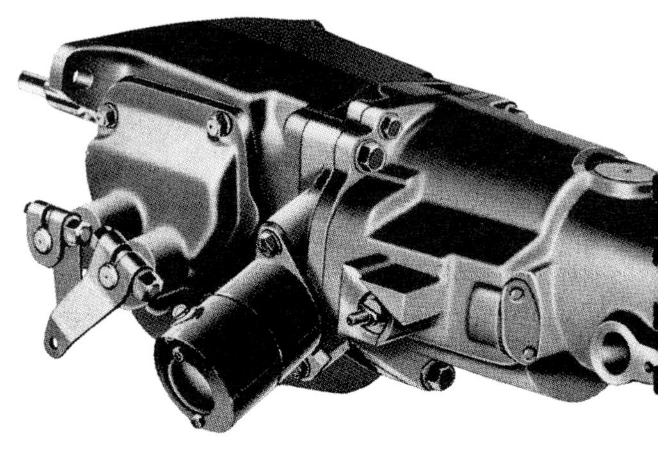

NEW TOUCH-DOWN
OVERDRIVE TRANSMISSION

Chevrolet's optional overdrive transmission is essentially a three-speed Synchro-Mesh transmission combined with a three-pinion planetary gear overdrive unit that provides a semi-automatic fourth speed. This fourth speed is inoperative when a simple T-handle control below the instrument panel is pulled out. But, while the handle is kept pushed in, the fourth speed is electrically controlled through the accelerator pedal, and the driver experiences many advantages unobtainable with a conventional transmission.

SIMPLIFIED SHIFTING IN TRAFFIC

With Overdrive, city driving is simplified. Below speeds of 30 m.p.h., the clutch pedal need be depressed only when starting from a standstill, or when the car is being brought to a stop. To shift, the driver simply releases the accelerator, moves the shift lever, and depresses the accelerator again.

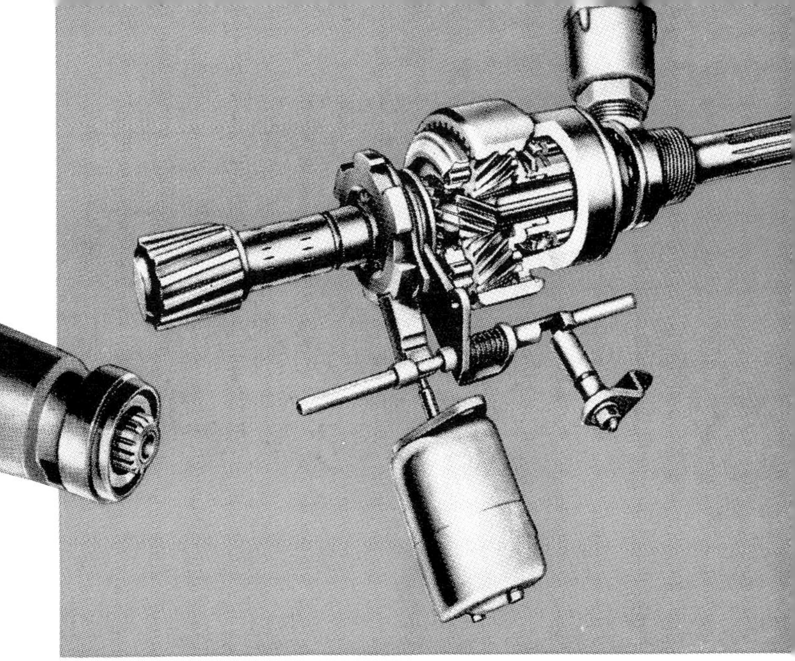

When the accelerator is momentarily released after the car speed reaches 30 m.p.h., the transmission automatically shifts into Overdrive. This stretches gasoline mileage, and also reduces engine wear and oil consumption, because Overdrive reduces engine speed more than 22 per cent for the same road speed with a conventional transmission. As an extra benefit, the slower-running engine operates smoother and quieter.

When the accelerator is fully depressed, extra power for rapid acceleration or hill climbing is immediately supplied — because the transmission automatically shifts into direct drive, supplying a safe reserve of power. Then, when the accelerator is momentarily released, Overdrive is re-engaged.

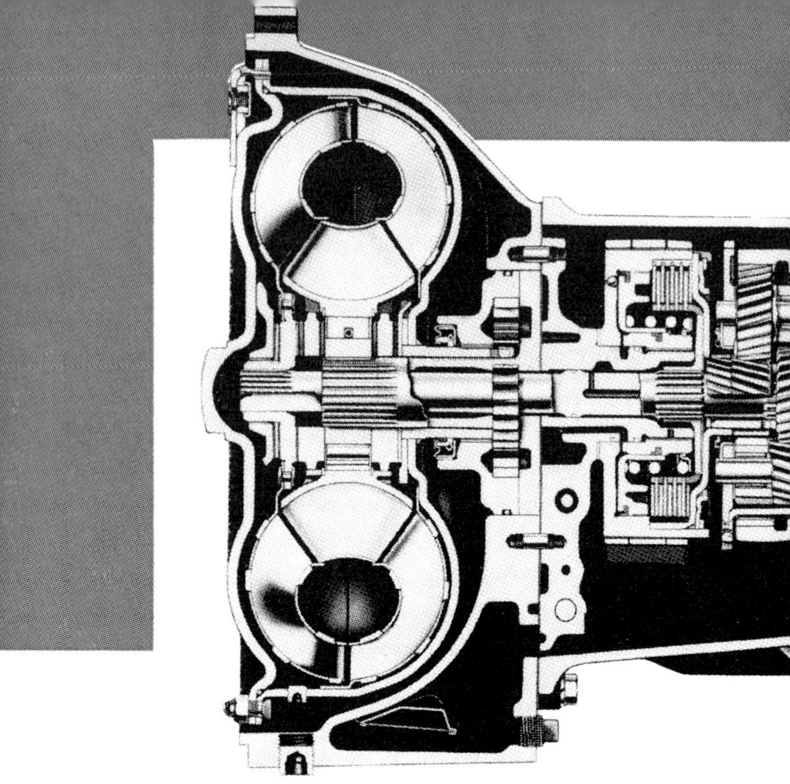

More than two million drivers enjoy the pleasure and convenience of automatic driving at its best . . . with all the brilliant acceleration, quiet, effortless cruising, and outstanding economy of operation that make Chevrolet's optional Powerglide transmission outstanding among all automatic transmissions. It's hard to believe that such a transmission could be improved. Yet, in its 1955 version, it's even smoother, more durable, and easier to service.

Basically, the transmission is a three-element hydraulic torque converter combined with a hydraulically-controlled planetary gearset for low speed and reverse operations. Much simpler than other types,

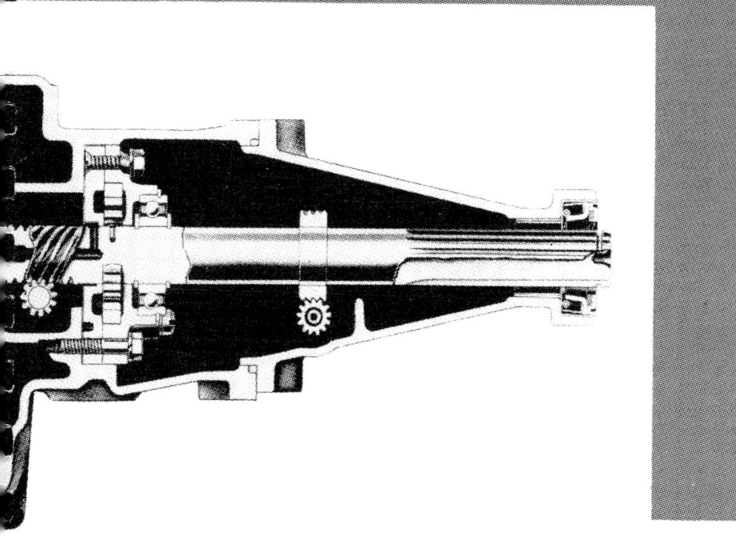

it has fewer parts that can go wrong and is easier to service. And, in operation, it's simpler than ABC . . . just step on the *A*ccelerator to go and on the *B*rake to stop. That's all! There is no *C*lutch!

Quickly responsive to the accelerator, the torque converter multiplies engine torque and transmits it to the wheels with oil smoothness—without the annoying jerks of multiple-step automatics. It performs more uniformly, too, because the oil is kept at the right operating temperature by controlled water-cooling. And when more power is needed, the planetary gears automatically provide a quick getaway at the traffic light, and fast acceleration for passing at speeds below approximately 50 m.p.h.

Other features are the parking lock for push-proof parking, starting in "Park" as well as in "Neutral," and the side-by-side locations of "Low" and "Reverse" for easy rocking out of sand or snow.

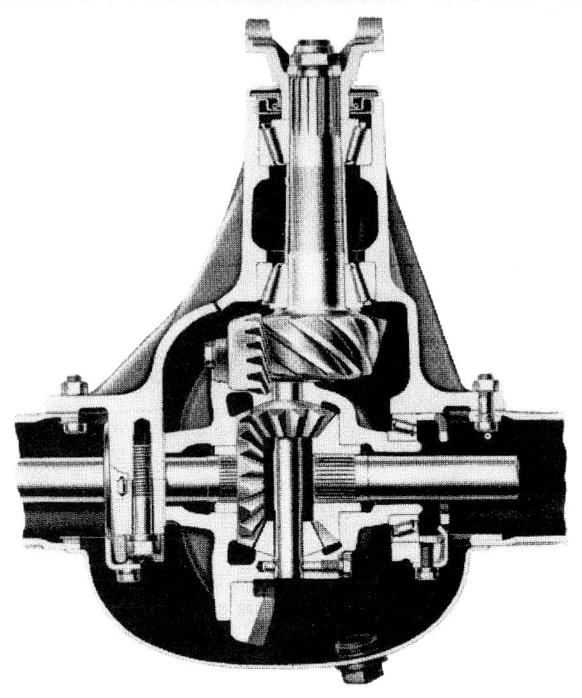

MORE DURABLE REAR AXLE

From the transmission, whichever it may be, the torque is transmitted through the new tubular propeller shaft and needle-bearing universal joints to the rear axle. This new Hotchkiss drive, adopted because it permits lower car height, also operates more smoothly and weighs less than the previous torque-tube drive.

The new axle is identical for all models, except for the ratios of the hypoid drive gears, which are varied to provide the best results from each power team. Completely reproportioned for greater torque capacity and greater durability, it has many detail changes that make it a better-performing, longer-lasting unit. Among the changes are new high-capacity pinion shaft roller bearings and ball-type wheel bearings, stronger structural members, and much improved oil sealing.

CONTROLS . . . Features

PERFECTED JUMBO DRUM BRAKES
- Large cast iron and steel drums.
- Self-energizing brake shoes; bonded linings.
- Hydraulic actuation. Optional power brakes.
- Exclusive braking dive control.
- Positive mechanical parking brakes.

BALL-RACE STEERING
- Spherical joint knuckles; relay-type linkage.
- Recirculating ball-nut steering gear.
- Optional power steering.

CONVENIENT HAND AND FOOT CONTROLS
- Large steering wheel; handy horn controls.
- Steering-column transmission control.
- Direct-pull parking brake and overdrive controls.
- Suspended brake and clutch pedals.
- Foot-controlled headlight dimmer switch.
- Complete lighting-system control switch.
- Windshield-wiper and accessory washer controls.
- Lighted key-turn ignition-starter switch.
- Built-in optional radio and heater controls.
- Individual controls for cowl side ventilators.

EASY-TO-READ INSTRUMENTS
- Extra-large speedometer with odometer.
- Gasoline and engine temperature gauges.
- Generator and oil-pressure indicator lights.
- Direction-signal indicator lights; lever control.
- Lighted automatic transmission selector dial.
- Instrument lights intensity control.

COMPLETE DRIVING VISION AIDS
- Full-width windshield defrosting.
- Dual windshield wipers (electric optional).
- Adjustable rearview mirror and sun shades.

NIGHT-CONTROL DRIVING LIGHTS
- Hooded headlights; with dual circuit breaker.
- Large, separate parking lights.
- Massive hooded tail-and-stop lights.
- Built-in accessory back-up lights.
- License plate lights in bumper guards.

UNSURPASSED EASE OF CONTROL!

CONTROL . . .

perfect control of car power

Whether a person has driven one mile, or a million, a wonderful new experience is in store for him behind the wheel of the Motoramic Chevrolet. Obedient to the slightest touch, this sure-footed new beauty threads its way smoothly through city traffic to the open road, setting new highs in responsiveness and roadability. Stops, at every speed, are quick and smooth, and remarkably level, and the car steers and parks with ball-bearing ease. Through all its paces, the new car handles with a smooth easiness such as is found in few other cars. The driver is in full control at all times, yet he drives relaxed, enjoying the finest driving he has ever done. And, with Chevrolet's op-

tional power assists—POWERGLIDE, POWER BRAKES, and POWER STEERING — driving is even easier.

NEW EASY-TO-READ INSTRUMENTS

Just sitting behind the steering wheel of a Motoramic Chevrolet is a thrilling experience, for straight ahead is the most sensible instrument cluster and control arrangement in the industry. The mammoth quadrant-shaped speedometer, with large white numerals on a black background, is fully visible through the steering wheel. Above it are the engine temperature and gasoline gauges, clearly labelled for split-second scanning. If the "country" headlight beams are on, if the oil pressure is low, or if the generator output drops below normal, one of three red lights gives a warning. When a turn is signalled, one of two green arrows flashes to indicate the direction of the turn.

And, in Powerglide models, the P-N-D-L-R selector dial is included with and lighted with the instruments. In this dial, the "P" stands for "Park." With the selector pointer in this position, the car will not move. Not all low-priced cars have this convenience. "N" is for "Neutral." The engine can be started in either "N" or "P"—another Chevrolet convenience. "D" is for "Drive," signifying the smoothest automatic driving. "L" is for "Low," used when the going is hard. "R," of course, means "Reverse," and it should be noted that, in the Chevrolet, "L" and "R" are side by side for easy rocking out of sand or snow.

FINEST INSTRUMENT LIGHTING

At night, when the driving lights are on, a soft, cool, green light illuminates all instrument dials. A simple turn of the main light switch adjusts its intensity to suit the driver's vision, or even turns it off. Radio and clock dials are lighted and controlled in the same way. As a safety measure, the hood above the cluster projects to guard against reflection of the instrument lights in the windshield.

Clustered within easiest reach around the instruments are the light switch, windshield wiper control, the combined key-turn ignition lock and starter switch and, in Bel Air and "Two-Ten" models, the cigarette lighter. All are clearly labelled. There is no choke control, because the choke is automatic.

The light switch knob controls every light in the car except, of course, the direction signals and lights that operate automatically.

Provision is made in the windshield-wiper control knob for the installation of a pushbutton that operates the accessory windshield washer. If the owner prefers, a pedal may be installed in the car, instead of the pushbutton, for foot control of the washer.

When the driving lights are switched on, the keyhole of the ignition lock and starter switch is illuminated, for easy key insertion. Exclusive to Chevrolet in its field is the unlocked "OFF" position of this switch. When the driver removes the key with the switch in this position, parking lot attendants can operate the car, but the locked glove compartment and trunk can't be opened.

The lighter is the handy electric pop-out type, with a shield around its element to catch burning tobacco fragments. Just below the lighter is a neat panel that may be removed for the installation of the optional heater and air conditioner controls. The concealed ash receptacle of the Bel Air and "Two-Ten" models is just to the right of this panel.

New controls for the parking brake and the optional overdrive transmission are located at the sides of the steering column, just below the instrument panel. Both are the pull-out type with T-shaped handles that are easy to grasp for a straight-back pull. The brake handle, now at the left, is pulled back to apply the brakes, and is released by turning it slightly and pushing it in to normal position. When the ignition is turned on, an accessory light, mounted on the in-

strument panel above the parking brake handle,
flashes a red warning that the brake is set. The
neat chrome-plated overdrive handle simply is pulled
out to disengage the unit and pushed in to engage it.

NEW STEERING COLUMN CONTROLS

The lever controls for the transmission and optional
direction signals are located just below the steering
wheel for easy finger-tip operation. All their mechanism is concealed in the new concentric steering
column.

The gearshift lever skims through its shifting pattern with easy smoothness, because of the perfection
of Chevrolet's remarkable Synchro-Mesh transmission. Of course, when the car is equipped with
Powerglide, the lever normally is kept in "Drive."

The direction signal lever is moved up or down respectively for right and left turns and, after a turn is
completed, automatically returns to neutral.

All the new steering wheels are fully a foot and a half in diameter and have deep finger notches on their undersides to assure a comfortable, firm grip no matter where the wheel may be held. Their recessed hubs not only look better but are out of the vision range of the instruments.

Chevrolet provides a full circle horn-blowing ring in Bel Air and "Two-Ten" models and a large horn button in "One-Fifty" models, to assure positive horn control at every position of the steering wheel. And, in the interest of greater safety, too, Chevrolet provides *two* matched horns in every model.

NEW VIBRATION-FREE PEDALS AND STEERING COLUMN

Every Chevrolet pedal is surfaced with a large grooved rubber pad to assure a firm, comfortable foot grip. Suspended mountings not only provide

more footroom on the toe panel but also eliminate holes in the panel. With these new suspensions, the linkages to the clutch, brakes, and carburetor are located higher to protect them better from road dirt and grime, and are designed to avoid the transmission of road sensations and engine vibrations to the driver's feet. Similarly, transmission of road shocks and vibrations to the steering wheel is averted. Another advantage of the suspended brake pedal is that, with this design, the brake master cylinder can be mounted in the engine compartment, high on the dash for easiest servicing. The only other standard foot control is the headlight beam switch located far to the left on the toe panel. With each press of the foot it switches the beams in city-country-city-country sequence.

When the car is equipped with power brakes, the brake pedal pad is located at about the same level as the accelerator pedal, so the driver can move his toe from the accelerator to the brake without lifting his heel from the floor.

NEW ALL-WEATHER DRIVING VISION

The crystal-clear Sweep-Sight windshield provides a
superior range of vision, for the safest, most pleas-
urable driving, and Chevrolet has taken every pre-
caution to maintain that vision in every kind of
weather. The sun shades can be quickly adjusted to
shield the driver's eyes from glare. In the Convertible they swivel up and down; in other models they
can be moved from the windshield to the side window and slid laterally on their shafts. This feature
even permits the lowered shades to be adjusted to
meet behind the rearview mirror to restrict glare at
any point across the windshield. For persons who
drive a great deal in sunlight, optional E-Z-Eye tinted
glass, with or without a dark tinted band at the top
of the windshield, not only reduces glare but makes
the car cooler. An accessory glare shield of light-
green transparent plastic also can be fitted to the
windshield. And as a protection against sun, rain.
and snow, a smart accessory sun visor can be
mounted outside above the windshield. Similar shields
of stainless steel are available for the side windows.

Two powerful windshield wipers, of the easily controlled vacuum type, are standard equipment on every model, but, for those who prefer them, two-speed electric wipers are available. The accessory windshield washer sprays liquid on the glass at the push of a button or pedal, so that the wiper blades can wipe cleanly without streaks. And, for completely automatic washing, there is an accessory washer-wiper coordinator. It sprays water, starts the blades, cleans the glass, and then parks the blades.

Under colder conditions, heat from Chevrolet's accessory heaters can be directed, full blast, for the full width of the windshield to clear the glass of frost, snow, and ice.

EXCELLENT REAR VISION

In every model, a clear-view rearview mirror is mounted inside above the center of the windshield. It may be set at any angle, and its offset mounting even permits it to be lowered to suit smaller persons. An accessory non-glare mirror may be substituted for the regular one. A flip of a tab on its lower edge changes the mirror from clear-view daytime vision to glare-proof nighttime vision. Another accessory mirror mounts outside the door to give a safe view of cars coming from behind on the left side. A second one also can be had for the right side of the car. Both are universally adjustable. For persons who don't wish to open the window to adjust the mirror, there's an accessory outside mirror that can be adjusted from inside the car.

NEW FOUR-FENDER VISIBILITY

Every fender can be clearly seen by the driver. Thus, with all corners of the car well marked, he can control his car better and drive more safely—without guesswork when driving in heavy traffic, maneuvering over winding country roads, or when parking.

NEW IMPROVED DRIVING LIGHTS

Even at night, all four fenders are visible for easier guiding of the car—because both the headlights and the tail lights are mounted high in the fender tops. These positions are important from a safety standpoint, too. Being located at the extremities of the car, the lights denote the car's width to other motorists, whether they are approaching from the front or the rear. And this feature is retained when the car is parked—because the extra-large parking lights, as well as the tail lights, are at the car corners. Then, too, when the car is parked with the lights off, ruby-red prisms in the tail lights glow in the glare of lights of cars coming up from behind. Another safety feature is the nighttime visibility of the tail lights from cars approaching from the sides.

In winter, the projecting hoods of both the headlights and the tail lights help to keep their lenses clear from snow and drippings that might ice the glass.

The headlights are the industry-sponsored sealed-beam type, but the Chevrolet lights are doubly protected by a dual circuit breaker in the lighting system.

This isolates the headlight circuit from the other circuits so that if a short develops in the other circuits, the headlights will continue to function.

The large rear lights not only house the tail and stop lights but also provide built-in provision for the installation of accessory back-up lights behind wide-angled lenses. The factory-installed accessory direction signal lights, of course, are built in both the parking and tail lights. The back-up lights go on automatically when the transmission is shifted into reverse.

The rear license plate, in its protected location on the rear deck, or in its recessed mounting in the bumper of station wagons, is illuminated by lights that are neatly built into the bumper guards.

The Motoramic Chevrolet is a dream to steer—easier, smoother, and safer than ever before. The compact design of the car contributes to its steering ability because it enables the Chevrolet to have a smaller turning diameter than other cars in its field. And the large over-all steering ratio (25.7 to 1) helps make the steering wheel easy to turn. But the major contributor to the wonderful steer-ability of the new car is its steering mechanism—new from road wheels to steering wheel.

At the wheels, the spherical joint steering knuckles turn easily. The relay-type linkage, which connects the wheels, has more rigid equal-length tie rods for better steering balance under all driving conditions. Self-adjusting spherical bearings throughout the linkage add to steering ease. And, exclusive in the low-price field is the Ball-Race steering gear, in which ball bearings eliminate nearly all friction. Even at the top of the steering column, there is a ball bearing that helps reduce steering effort.

Never before has Chevrolet offered a steering system that operates so easily and safely.

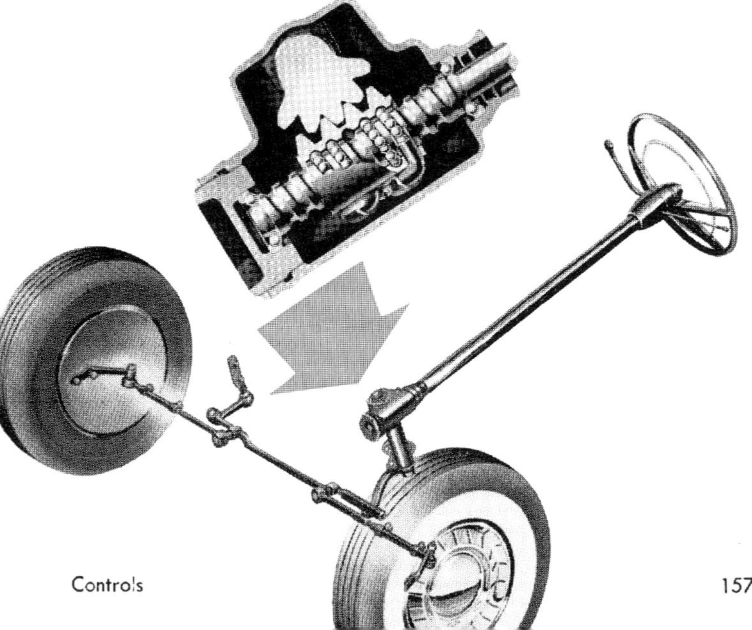

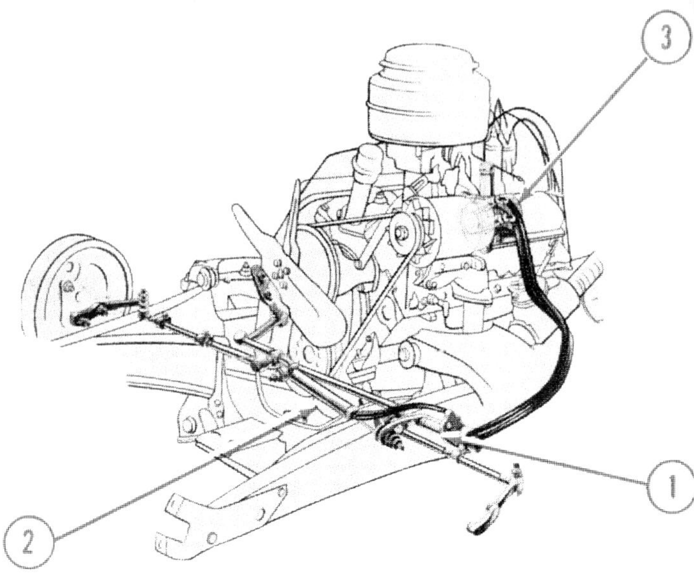

NEW LINKAGE-TYPE POWER STEERING

But wonderful as it is, Chevrolet's steering can be made even easier with Chevrolet's new Power-Touch steering option. Because of Chevrolet's completely new steering linkage, it was possible to design right into that linkage a new type of power steering that retains all the driver advantages of the previous design yet is simpler, easier to service, and within the purse-range of more people.

The new unit features the direct action principle. All its components are now located in the part of the steering linkage where they are most effective. The hydraulic control valve (1) and hydraulic power cylinder (2) are connected directly to the steering relay link. Hence, road shocks are cushioned by the cylinder before ever reaching the driver's hands. Whenever more than *three* pounds of effort is required, the power steering begins to function and provides up to 80 per cent assistance in steering the car. A new vane-type pressure supply pump (3) produces hydraulic pressure of over 750 pounds whenever required—for effortless parking, and driving that's more relaxing, more enjoyable.

VELVET-PRESSURE JUMBO-DRUM BRAKES

Chevrolet's Jumbo-Drum brakes are self-energizing, which means that when the pedal is pressed, little driver effort is required because the turning drums move the brake shoes so that they wedge against the drums. The eleven-inch diameter drums are made with steel sides and cast iron braking surfaces that dissipate the heat of braking rapidly. Bonded brake shoe linings last up to twice as long as the out-moded riveted type.

Sealing against dirt and splash protects the linings so that stops are always effective.

A fully mechanical system that's entirely separate from the hydraulic braking system applies the two rear-wheel brakes when the parking brake handle is pulled back. Both rear wheels remain braked even when one is jacked up to change a tire.

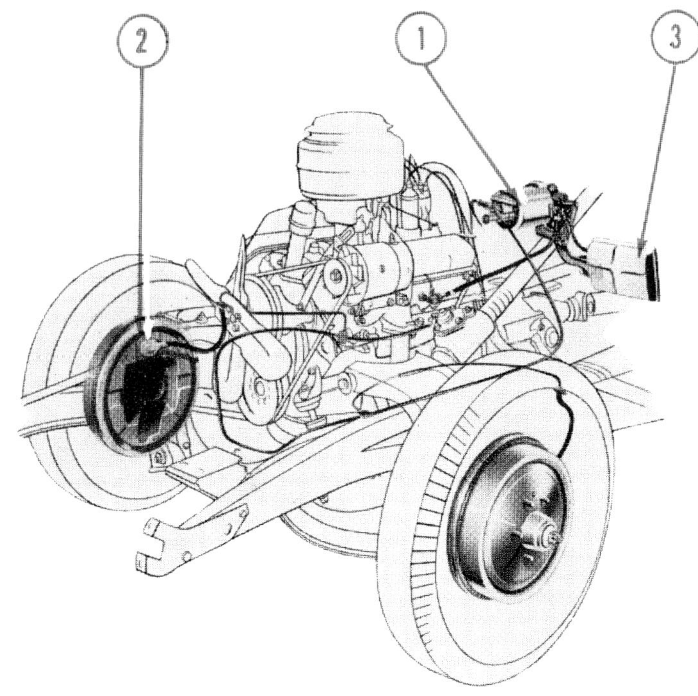

NEW POWER BRAKE OPTION

Chevrolet Power Brakes do up to one-third of the work of stopping. Just a gentle toe-tip pressure, and the car stops quietly, smoothly. They work easier, but the driver still retains the familiar feel of complete stopping control.

Their new design is simplicity itself. A vacuum-power cylinder (1) supplies the added power which exerts pressure on (2) the car's hydraulic braking system. A reserve tank (3) assures a vacuum reserve even when the engine is not running.

The Motoramic Chevrolet is the *only* car that offers the comfort—and safety—of controlled braking action. This exclusive feature is engineered into Chevrolet's unique new spherical joint front suspension. The scientifically inclined control arms of the suspension produce a lifting effect that counteracts "nosing down" during normal braking to assure "heads up" stops, thereby adding to passenger comfort and reducing the possibility of locking bumpers in traffic.

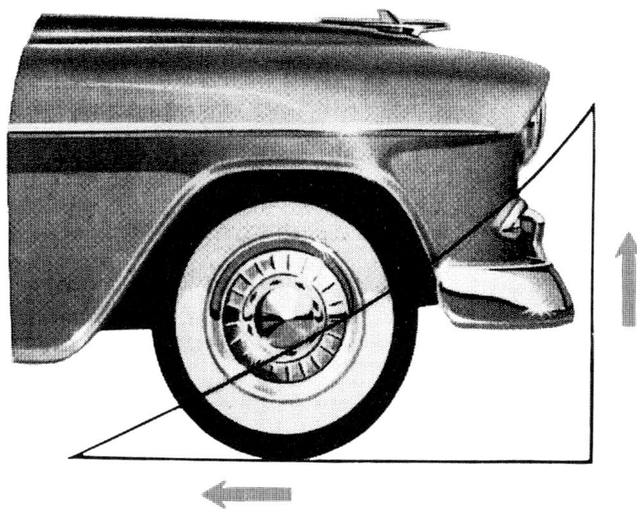

THAT'S IT!

. . . THE STORY OF THE

ALL-NEW MOTORAMIC

CHEVROLET!

In the preceding sections of this book, all the facts a salesman needs to advise his customers in selecting Chevrolets have been described in simple everyday language and in a sensible sequence.

In every section, many illustrations enable him to show the details of Chevrolet design to his customers as he describes its features to them. And in nearly every section, too, one or more two-page illustrations of the subject matter list its more important selling points.

To jog his memory, the first page of each section lists the features covered in the section. Put together, these first pages comprise a complete list of features of the new car . . . and, to assist him further, all the facts are repeated again in the next section of this book, *in alphabetical sequence,* so he can find them fast.

FAST FACTS

Features and specifications of Chevrolet cars and their equipment—standard, optional, and accessory—briefly expressed and in alphabetical order.

For uniformity, each item is listed by its functional name. For instance, the front suspension system is listed as "Front Suspension" instead of "Knee-Action."

Definitions

STANDARD EQUIPMENT: That equipment which is included in the list price of the car.

OPTIONAL EQUIPMENT: That equipment which is installed at the factory, at the customer's request, in addition to or in place of standard equipment—at extra cost.

ACCESSORY EQUIPMENT: That equipment which is installed by the dealer (or the customer), at the customer's request, in addition to or in place of standard equipment—at extra cost.

CHROME: Items described as "chrome" are either chrome-plated metal or stainless steel.

PERFECTION IN EVERY DETAIL!

AIR CLEANER, CARBURETOR: Oil-wetted type for 6-cylinder engines. One-pint oil-bath type for V8 (optional for 6-cylinder engines). Both are combined with flame arrester and silencer.

AIR CONDITIONER: Compact, single-unit, all-weather air conditioner by Frigidaire—optional for V8 models except Convertible. Unit installs at front of car, leaving luggage compartment unobstructed.

ARM RESTS: Door-pull arm rests on all doors of Bel Air and "Two-Ten" models, except rear doors of station wagons. Rear-seat arm rests in all Bel Air and "Two-Ten" sedans and coupes. Bel Air arm rests are built-in type, except in rear of 2-door sedan; Bel Air 2-door sedan rear-seat arm rests and all "Two-Ten" arm rests are applied type. Applied door-pull arm rests are available as accessories, front and/or rear, for "One-Fifty" models.

ASH RECEPTACLES: Concealed instrument panel ash bin of tilting type, standard in Bel Air and "Two-Ten" models and available as an accessory for "One-Fifty" models. Tilting bin type in center of front-seat back rest in Bel Air and "Two-Ten" 4-door sedans. Bin type with snap cover integral with each rear-seat arm rest of Bel Air and "Two-Ten" 2-door sedans and coupes. All ash receptacles have built-in snuffers and are removable for cleaning.

ASSIST STRAPS: Two loop type assist straps in Bel Air and "Two-Ten" 2-door sedans and in Delray Club Coupe.

AXLE: See Rear Axle.

BACK-UP LIGHTS: Accessory lights, in tail-and-stop-light units, light automatically when car is shifted into reverse.

BATTERY: 12-volt, 54-plate battery (50 ampere-hour rating at 20 hours), located under hood at right side of engine. Red indicator light, in instrument cluster (at left), lights when generator is not charging.

BEARINGS: See Camshaft, Crankshaft, Engine Bearings, Wheels.

BODY CONSTRUCTION: Fisher Unisteel (all-steel, all-welded) construction. Turret top braced by central bow (except fabric top for Convertible), full-length underbody (floor), double-walled cowl with welded-in instrument panel, unitized sides with integral rear fenders, double-walled full-panel doors, double-walled trunk lid (sedans and coupes), box-section lift gate and double-walled full-panel tail gate (station wagons).

BODY INSULATION: Thorough insulation and sound deadening of top, floor, dash and cowl, rear quarter panels, load compartments, wheelhouses, doors, and rear closures. Additional sound deadener in Bel Air and "Two-Ten" steel tops.

BODY INTERIOR: See Interior.

BODY MOUNTING: 14 rubber cushions, insulating body from chassis. Front end structure, including fenders and hood, is integrated with body and supported at front on one central rubber cushion.

BODY SEALING: Permanent rubber sealing of all stationary windows; rubber-backed, fabric-lined window glass run channels; compressed rubber seals around doors, ventipanes, rear closures, and at front of Convertible top.

BORE AND STROKE: 6-cylinder engines, 3.56" x 3.94"; V8, 3.75" x 3.00".

BRAKES: 4-wheel self-energizing service brakes. Bonded linings of full-molded asbestos composition; 158 sq. in. total effective area. 11" dia. drums with cast alloy iron braking surfaces. Hydraulic application. Master cylinder on dash for easy servicing. Also see Parking Brakes, Power Brakes, and Pedals.

BRAKING DIVE: Controlled by suspension system.

BUMPERS: Chrome, contoured wraparound bumpers with anti-lock guards, solidly mounted to chassis frame at front and rear. Rear bumpers of station wagons are indented at center for mounting of license plate. Accessory chrome radiator grille guard and front and rear fender guards mount on standard bumpers.

CAMSHAFT: Cast alloy iron. Special high-lift cams in 136-hp Six, for deeper engine "breathing." Four bearings in 6-cylinder engines; 5 in V8.

CAMSHAFT DRIVE: Fabric composition and steel timing gears (6-cylinder engines); silent chain and sprocket drive (V8).

CARBURETOR: Downdraft carburetion. Single concentric carburetor (6-cylinder engines); dual carburetor, or optional 4-barrel carburetor with dual exhaust system, (V8).

CARPETS: See Floor Coverings.

CHOKE: Automatic type; integral with carburetor.

CHROME, BODY INTERIOR: Bel Air models—Instrument panel center; instrument cluster and clock frames; radio speaker frame; "Bel Air" on speaker and steering wheel hub emblem (gold plate); horn blowing ring; front-seat adjustment knob and scuff pad molding; side wall scuff pad moldings; door and window controls, light frames; door sill plates (etched aluminum), plus roof bows and rails and rear window molding in Sport Coupe, and windshield garnish molding in Convertible. • "Two-Ten" models—Instrument cluster frame and radio speaker frame; "Chevrolet" on speaker; steering wheel hub emblem; horn blowing ring; front-seat adjustment knob and scuff pad molding; side wall moldings; door and window controls; light frame; and door sill plates (etched aluminum). • "One-Fifty" models—Instrument cluster frame; radio speaker frame; "Chevrolet" on speaker; horn button emblem; front-seat adjustment knob; door and window controls; light frame; and door sill plates (etched aluminum).

CHROME, FRONT OF CAR: Hood ornament, frame for plastic hood emblem, headlight and parking light rims; radiator grille, and bumper and guards; windshield reveal and pillar moldings and rearview mirror back on Bel Air models; windshield reveal on "Two-Ten" models.

CHROME, REAR OF CAR: Window reveal (Bel Air and "Two-Ten" sedans and coupes, except Convertible), window top and belt moldings (Bel

Air and "Two-Ten" station wagons), frame for plastic Chevrolet emblem, light frames, "V" insignia on fender ends for models with V8 engine, bumpers and guards, and station wagon tail gate handle.

CHROME, SIDE OF CAR: Bel Air sedans and coupes—Ventipane frames, window top (except Convertible) and sill moldings, door handles, front fender "windsplit" moldings, sash moldings, rear quarter moldings with white center and Bel Air name and crest, and wheel disks. • "Two-Ten" sedans and coupes—Ventipane frames, window sill moldings, door handles, "Chevrolet" on front fenders, sash moldings, rear-quarter moldings, and hub caps. • Bel Air and "Two-Ten" station wagons —Same as sedans in respective series except for special window top and belt moldings extending around the sides and rear and special winged spearheads replacing the sash moldings. • "One-Fifty" Models—Ventipane frames, door handles, "Chevrolet" on front fenders, and hub caps.

CLOCK: Electric, self-starting precision timepiece with sapphire-jeweled movement and illuminated dial, on radio speaker of Bel Air models. Accessory for "Two-Ten" and "One-Fifty" models.

CLUTCH: Diaphragm spring type with permanently lubricated ball throwout (release) bearing and strap drive; 9½" dia. single dry plate disk, with 6-cylinder engine, 10" dia. with V8. Coil springs at hub of disk serve as torsion dampers. Optional 11" dia. heavy-duty clutch for engines with Synchro-Mesh transmission.

CLUTCH PEDAL: See Pedals.

COAT HOOKS: Two chrome hooks in rear compartment of Bel Air and "Two-Ten" 4-door sedans and station wagons, 2-door sedans, and Club Coupe.

COLORS: Wide selection of exterior colors in solid, optional two-tone, and optional special two-tone treatments, depending on model (190 model-color combinations). See Models section, pages 42-43.

COLORS, INTERIOR: See Models section.

COMPASS: Accessory illuminated compass mounted in center on top of instrument panel.

CONVERTIBLE TOP: Folding top of chevrolon, a special weatherproof convertible-top fabric, in blue, green, beige, or vinyl-coated white, with zippered-in vinyl plastic rear window; tailored to all-steel articulating framework. Folds completely into well behind rear seat and is covered by snapped-on vinyl boot that matches seat upholstery. Automatic hydraulically operated folding mechanism controlled from instrument panel. Accessory moisture-sensitive automatic top raiser causes top to lift and unfold when rain starts.

COMBUSTION CHAMBERS: High-turbulence type, assuring most complete combustion of fuel mixture; of special wedge shape in V8.

COMPRESSION RATIO: 6-cylinder engines, 7.5 to 1; V8, 8.0 to 1.

CONNECTING RODS: Drop-forged alloy steel of I-section.

COOLING SYSTEM: See Engine Cooling System and Radiator.

COURTESY LIGHTS: Lights under instrument panel light automatically when either front door is opened. Standard in Convertible; accessory in other models.

COWL: See Body Construction and Ventilation.

CRANKSHAFT: Precision-counterbalanced, drop-forged alloy steel crankshaft with rubber-floated vibration damper. Four bearings in 6-cylinder engines; five in V8.

CYLINDER BLOCK AND HEAD MATERIAL: Cast alloy iron.

D

DEFROSTER: See Heater.

DIRECTION SIGNALS: Accessory lights, installed at the factory in parking and tail-and-stop-light units; operated by lever on left of steering column. In operation, the lights on "turn" side of car and a corresponding green arrow on instrument panel flash intermittently. Self-cancellation occurs when turn is completed.

DISPLACEMENT, PISTON: 6-cylinder engines, 235.5 cu. in; V8, 265.0 cu. in.

DOME LIGHT: See Interior Lights.

DOOR EDGE GUARDS: Accessory chrome strip moldings on vertical rear edges of doors; for all sedans and coupes.

DOOR HANDLES, OUTSIDE: Chrome, stationary, grip type, with pushbutton releases. Accessory chrome shields, installed between handles and door surfaces.

DOOR SILL PLATES: Wide etched aluminum plates protecting full sills of all doors.

DOORS: Double-walled full-panel front-opening doors, with concealed hinges (offset hinges on front doors); positive door checks, holding doors in full open position; rotary locks; chrome outside handles shielding pushbutton lock releases; lever inside release handles; door-pull arm rests (in Bel Air and "Two-Ten" models); separate, weather-protected key locks in both front doors below handles; plastic button-on-sill inside latches, with safety adjustment for rear doors, permitting keyless door locking; one key for operating all car locks.

DOOR WINDOWS: See Windows, Door.

DRIP MOLDINGS: See Top, Turret.

DRIVE SYSTEM: See Propeller Shaft.

DRUMS, BRAKE: See Brakes.

ELECTRICAL SYSTEM: See Engine Electrical System.

ENGINE: 6-cylinder or 8-cylinder, high-compression, valve-in-head engine—123-hp Six, 136-hp Six (with optional Powerglide automatic transmission only), 162-hp V8, or optional 180-hp V8 (with 4-barrel carburetor and dual exhaust system).

ENGINE BEARINGS: Pressure-lubricated, precision-interchangeable, thin-wall, steel backed babbitt crankshaft, camshaft, and connecting rod bearings.

ENGINE COOLING SYSTEM: Staggered 4-blade fan; self-adjusting, permanently-lubricated water pump; thermostat and by-pass temperature control; full-length water jackets around all cylinders.

ENGINE ELECTRICAL SYSTEM: 12-volt system. 54-plate battery (50 ampere-hour rating at 20 hours). 25-ampere generator, with current and voltage regulators. Solenoid-operated positive-shift starter. All-weather ignition. Automatic centrifugal and vacuum spark advance control. Also see Spark Plugs.

ENGINE FUEL SYSTEM: Pulsator-type mechanical fuel pump driven by camshaft; downdraft carburetor with automatic choke; air cleaner; automatic fuel mixture heat control; high-turbulence combustion chambers.

ENGINE LUBRICATION SYSTEM: Controlled full-pressure feed lubrication system. Gear pump with floating oil intake. Crankcase breather cap.

ENGINE MOUNTING: Power plant dynamically balanced on four rubber cushions—two at front and two at rear.

ENGINE VENTILATION: Road draft at end of ventilator tube sucks harmful fumes from engine and exhausts them below car.

EXHAUST SYSTEM: See Muffler.

FAN: See Engine Cooling System.

FENDERS: High-crowned front and rear fenders, clearly visible from driver's seat. Front fenders horizontally ribbed with "windsplit" lines. Rear fenders integral with body structure. Wheel openings flanged for stiffness.

FENDER SHIELDS: Accessory chrome shields mounted on front fenders, behind wheel openings; may be used in combination with accessory chrome body sill moldings.

FILTERS: See Fuel Tank or Oil Filter.

FINISH, EXTERIOR: Nine-step finishing process —1. Alkaline cleaning and rust proofing. 2. Primer coat. 3. Glaze coat. 4. Wet sanding. 5, 6 and 7.

Three double coats of pyroxylin lacquer. 8. Sound deadener application. 9. Machine polishing. See Colors also.

FLOOR: All-steel floor, with integral toe pan and embossed rear seat foot rest, reinforced by pressed-in ribs and box-section cross beams and sills. Thoroughly insulated, and covered with carpets or rubber mats. Use of suspended pedals eliminates openings in floor, for better sealing.

FLOOR COVERINGS: Bel Air sedans and coupes and "Two-Ten" Delray Club Coupe—Colored deep-pile carpet. "Two-Ten" sedans, and Bel Air and "Two-Ten" station wagons—Colored rubber mats. "One-Fifty" models—Black rubber mats, including mat on floor of load space in Utility Sedan. Sedan and coupe trunk—Black rubber mat. Station wagon load compartment floor—Beige ribbed linoleum on platform, tail gate, and exposed surfaces of folded rear seat. Accessory rubber floor mats for individual car occupants; in black, blue, brown, red, or green.

FLYWHEEL: Cast alloy iron flywheel (reinforced pressed steel flywheel with automatic transmission). Hardened steel ring gear.

FOOT RESTS: Solid, comfortably angled front seat toe pan and rear seat foot rest formed in floor.

FRAME, CHASSIS: Double-drop box-girder frame (with special X-structure of I-beams in Convertible).

FRONT SUSPENSION: Independent wheel suspension with coil springs of chrome alloy steel and coaxial, life-sealed, direct, double-acting shock absorbers. Self-adjusting spherical-joint steering knuckles with non-metallic bearing liners. Four lubrication fittings.

FUEL: Engines are designed to operate efficiently on regular grades of gasoline but, under some conditions, such as high temperature or deposit accumulation, smoother performance may be obtained with premium grades. The compression ratio of the V8 is sufficiently high to fully utilize the higher octane value of premium fuel.

FUEL TANK: 16-gallon (17-gallon, station wagons) fuel tank, with large capacity filter screen, and hip-high filler concealed behind door, with over-center spring, in side of left rear fender. Electrically operated dial indicator, in instrument cluster, is indirectly lighted by instrument lights. Accessory chrome filler door guard protects bottom and rear edge of door opening in fender. Accessory filler cap with key lock safeguards gasoline.

GASOLINE: See Fuel.

GATE, STATION WAGON LIFT: High-lifting box-section gate, framing rear window. Two concealed hinges. Chrome, self-latching, telescoping type support at each side. Wedge, at center, engaged by dovetail on tail gate, holds lift gate securely locked.

GATE, STATION WAGON TAIL: Double-walled full-panel gate with two hinges. Support cables at sides hold gate level with load compartment floor; are provided with springs that re-wind the cables while gate is being closed. Slam latches at sides are operated by chrome central outside T-handle, with integral weather-protected key lock. Plastic "Chevrolet" emblem with chrome frame is mounted on center of gate. Inside gate surface is covered with durable linoleum. Gate height from ground, approximately 30" (unloaded).

GENERATOR: 25-ampere air-cooled generator with current and voltage regulators. Optional 30-ampere generator. Optional 40-ampere low-cut-in generator.

GLASS: See Window Glass.

GLOVE COMPARTMENT: Fully lined central glove compartment with pushbutton key lock. Automatic light standard in Bel Air and "Two-Ten" models, accessory in "One-Fifty" models.

GOVERNOR, ENGINE: Optional velocity type governor, between carburetor and intake manifold; available with 123-hp Six to restrict maximum car speed to 35 mph.

GRILLE: See Radiator Grille.

HEADLIGHTS: Hooded sealed-beam headlights with chrome rims; protected by dual circuit breakers. Foot switch at left of toe pan is depressed to switch from city to country beams. Red warning light, at speedometer center, lights when country beams are on. Wide spacing of headlights denotes car width clearly.

HEADLINING: See Interior Finishing Materials.

HEATER: Optional de luxe heater and defroster unit controlled from illuminated control panel on instrument panel. Optional recirculating heater and defroster unit with switch on instrument panel and defroster adjustment on unit.

HEIGHT, CAR LOADED: Sedans, 60.5"; Delray Club Coupe, 60.5"; Sport Coupe, 59.1"; Convertible, 59.1"; Station Wagons, 60.8".

HOOD: Front-opening reinforced one-piece hood panel with gear type hinges, double-acting counter-balancing hinge springs, and slam latch with safety catch. Latch, at front of hood, slightly to the right of center, may be unlatched and hood lifted with one hand in one continuous motion. Colorful plastic hood emblem in chrome frame; chrome hood ornament with eagle motif.

HORNS: Two matched vibrator type horns, in engine compartment, controlled by chrome full-circle horn blowing ring in Bel Air and "Two-Ten" models; by horn button on steering wheel hub in "One-Fifty" models.

HORSEPOWER, MAXIMUM: 6-cylinder engine with Synchro-Mesh transmission (with or without overdrive), 123 hp at 3800 rpm; 6-cylinder engine with Powerglide automatic transmission, 136 hp at 4200 rpm; V8 with Synchro-Mesh transmission (with or without overdrive) or with Powerglide automatic transmission, 162 hp at 4400 rpm; V8 with optional 4-barrel carburetor and dual exhaust system, 180 hp at 4600 rpm.

HOTCHKISS DRIVE: Tubular propeller shaft, with two needle-bearing universal joints, transmits engine turning force from transmission to rear axle.

HUB CAPS: See Wheel Disks.

IGNITION: All-weather type with hermetically sealed coil, high-tower distributor, and neoprene spark plug caps. Non-metallic ignition cable, with linen core impregnated with electrical conducting material, and insulated with rubber and neoprene jacket.

IGNITION-STARTER SWITCH: 4-position type (locked off, unlocked off, on, and start) at right of steering column; operated by integral knob or by car key. Key-turn starter returns to "on" position automatically when released. Keyhole is lighted when car lights are on.

INSTRUMENT CLUSTER: Quadrant-shaped cluster, high on instrument panel, directly in front of driver, includes: speedometer with odometer; gasoline gauge; engine temperature indicator; generator charge, oil pressure, and country beam warning lights; and direction signal arrows.

INSTRUMENT LIGHTS: Indirect instrument lighting in soft green; may be dimmed or turned off by turning main light switch knob. Clock and radio dials have same type of light and control.

INSTRUMENT PANEL: Welded-in wraparound instrument panel with lockable central glove compartment, and quadrant-shaped instrument cluster in front of driver, balanced by radio speaker of same shape. Two-tone color treatment. Bel Air equipment includes automatic glove compartment light, built-in ash receptacle, cigarette lighter and electric clock. "Two-Ten" equipment includes automatic glove compartment light, built-in ash receptacle, and cigarette lighter.

INSULATION: See Body Insulation.

INTERIOR COLORS: Two-tone interior color schemes, keyed to exterior colors. See Models section.

INTERIOR FINISHING MATERIALS: Bel Air sedans—Combination of pattern cloth, gabardine flat cloth, and vinyl seat upholstery; gabardine flat cloth and vinyl side wall covering; plain napped cloth headlining and sun shade covering. • Sport

Coupe—Combination of straw pattern cloth and vinyl seat upholstery; vinyl side wall covering, and vinyl headlining and sun shade covering. • Convertible—All-vinyl seat upholstery, side wall covering, and sun shade covering. • "Two-Ten" sedans—Combination of pattern cloth, ripple-weave gabardine, and vinyl seat upholstery; vinyl side wall covering; and plain napped cloth headlining and sun shade covering. • Club Coupe—All-vinyl seat upholstery, side wall covering, headlining, and sun shade covering. • "One-Fifty" sedans—Combination of pattern cloth and vinyl seat upholstery, vinyl side wall covering, and plain napped cloth headlining and sun shade covering. Load space behind seat in Utility Sedan is finished with composition board walls. • Bel Air 4-door station wagon—Combination of straw pattern cloth and vinyl seat upholstery; vinyl side wall covering; and vinyl headlining and sun shade covering. • "Two-Ten" and "One-Fifty" station wagons—All-vinyl seat upholstery, side wall covering, headlining, and sun shade covering.

INTERIOR LIGHTS: Central dome light in sedans, Club Coupe, and station wagons; two rear corner lights in Sport Coupe; two courtesy lights under instrument panel in Convertible. Manual control by main light switch on instrument panel. Jamb switches, automatically operating lights when doors are opened, provided at all doors of Bel Air models and at both front doors of "Two-Ten" models. Chrome light frames; plastic lenses.

JACK: Bumper type; 1200 lb. capacity. Jack handle combined with wheel wrench. Rattle-free stowage of spare wheel, jack, and jack handle. Accessory tool kit.

KEY: See Locks, Key.

LENGTH, CAR OVERALL: Sedans and coupes, 195.6"; station wagons, 197.1".

LICENSE PLATE FRAME: Accessory telescoping chrome frame, adjustable to fit all sizes of license plates.

LICENSE PLATE MOUNTING: Sedan and coupes —On trunk lid below handle. Station wagons—On indentation in center of rear bumper. Plate is lighted by two lights housed in bumper guards.

LIFT GATE, STATION WAGON: See Gate.

LIGHTER, CIGARETTE: Electric pop-out type, with ash shield on element, on instrument panel of Bel Air and "Two-Ten" models. Accessory for "One-Fifty" models.

LIGHTS: Listed under individual names.

LIGHT SWITCH, MAIN: Push-pull knob at left of steering column controls all standard car lights; pulls out to light instrument and driving lights; rotates clockwise to control instrument light intensity and counterclockwise to turn on interior light.

LININGS, BRAKE: See Brakes.

LOAD SPACE, SEDAN AND COUPE: See Trunk.

LOAD SPACE, STATION WAGON: Flat load platform, extended by folding rear seat, and/or lowering tail gate. Beige ribbed linoleum on platform, tail gate, and exposed surfaces of folded seat. 87 cu. ft. capacity (from floor to window sills, with seat folded). Length 47" with seat in use, 84.4" with seat folded, 106.1" with seat folded and tail gate down; width 58.3"; height 36.9". Rear opening width, 43.6"; height, 28.3"; height of tail gate to ground (unloaded), approx. 30". Section of platform lifts out for access to spare wheel-well below platform. Chrome binding at platform ends; and around wheel-well in Bel Air Station Wagon.

LOAD SPACE, UTILITY SEDAN: Load space behind front seat, reached by folding center-fold halves of seat back rest. Flat platform with black rubber mat. Black composition-board walls. 31 cu. ft. capacity from floor to window sills, in addition to 20 cu. ft. trunk capacity.

LOCKS, KEY: Weather-protected key locks for both front doors and trunk or station wagon end gates. Key-turn starter and ignition lock switch. Pushbutton key lock for glove compartment. One master key operates all car locks.

LUBRICATION: See Engine Lubrication System, Front Suspension, and Oil.

MIRROR, REARVIEW: Top-mounted universally-adjustable inside type. Accessory rearview mirrors include inside prismatic (non-glare) type, outside remote control type that mounts through left door and is controlled from inside car, and outside universally-adjustable type that can be mounted on left side or both side doors. Another outside mirror is built into the accessory spot light.

MIRROR, VANITY: Accessory make-up mirror; clips to back of either sun shade.

MODELS: See Models section, page 6.

MUFFLER: 30" reverse flow muffler with three sound-deadening chambers. Special 24" muffler in Convertible. Muffler tailpipe end coated with aluminum to prevent rusting. Accessory chrome tailpipe extension. Optional dual exhaust for V8.

OCTANE SELECTOR: Adjustment at ignition distributor permits regulation of spark timing to provide best engine performance with each grade of gasoline.

OIL CAPACITY, CRANKCASE: 5 qt. for refill (6-cylinder engine); 4 qt. (V8). When oil filter is used, an additional quart of oil is required.

OIL FILLER, CRANKCASE: At front of engine on top of valve rocker cover (6-cylinder engines); high on left front of engine (V8).

OIL FILTER: Optional one-quart-capacity unit; for use in dusty air.

OIL PAN: Incorporates welded-in baffle which prevents oil surging on quick stops and reduces possibility of oil foaming.

OIL PRESSURE INDICATOR: Red warning light, in instrument cluster (at right), lights when oil pressure is low.

OIL PUMP: High capacity gear type with floating oil intake.

OPTIONAL EQUIPMENT AND ACCESSORIES: Listed in the Models section, pages 46-47.

OVERDRIVE: See Transmission, Overdrive.

PACKAGE SHELF: Deep and broad shelf below window behind rear seat in all sedans and coupes except Convertible.

PAINT: Pyroxylin lacquer. See Colors, Finish, or list of colors in Models section, pages 42-43.

PARKING BRAKES: Mechanical actuation of rear service brakes through steel cables. Direct-pull T-handle control, at left of steering column, is turned 60° counter-clockwise to release brakes. Accessory red warning signal, under instrument panel, lights automatically when ignition is turned on and flashes until brakes are released.

PARKING LIGHTS: Two, at each side of radiator grille below headlights. Chrome rims.

PASSENGER CAPACITY: Six, except five in Convertible and three in Utility Sedan.

PEDAL, ACCELERATOR: Rubber-padded accelerator treadle operates push rod extending through dash panel. Accessory rubber treadle cover, with integral heel pad, saves wear of floor covering.

PEDALS, BRAKE AND CLUTCH: Rubber-padded, swing-type, suspended brake and clutch pedals allow more foot room and eliminate holes in toe pan, for better sealing.

PISTON DISPLACEMENT: See Displacement.

PISTON PINS: Chromium steel pins, locked (6-cylinder engines) or pressed (V8) in connecting rod ends; offset to insure quiet operation.

PISTON RINGS: Two compression rings and one oil control ring above each piston pin. Compression rings are of thick-wall twist type. Oil control ring is wide-slot type with expander in 6-cylinder engines with conventional transmission; is multi-piece type in 136-hp Six and in V8.

PISTONS: Lightweight cast aluminum alloy with integral steel struts to control expansion; surfaces tin coated to resist wear.

PLENUM CHAMBER: See Ventilation.

POWER BRAKES: Optional low-pedal vacuum-power service brake control, with pedal on same level of operation as accelerator pedal; vacuum power does up to one-third of the work of braking.

POWERGLIDE: See Transmission, Automatic

POWER STEERING: Optional linkage-type hydraulic power steering control. Assistance starts at 3 pounds steering wheel rim pull; reaches 80% at 8 pounds.

POWER TEAMS: 123-hp Six with Synchro-Mesh transmission and 3.70 to 1 ratio rear axle. 123-hp Six with overdrive transmission and 4.11 to 1 ratio rear axle. 136-hp Six with Powerglide automatic transmission and 3.55 to 1 ratio rear axle. 162-hp V8* with Synchro-Mesh transmission and 3.70 to 1 ratio rear axle. 162-hp V8* with overdrive transmission and 4.11 to 1 ratio rear axle. 162-hp V8* with Powerglide automatic transmission and 3.55 to 1 ratio rear axle.—*V8 horsepower is increased to 180 when optional 4-barrel carburetor and dual exhaust system are used.

PROPELLER SHAFT: Precision-balanced tubular type with two universal joints (Hotchkiss drive).

RADIATOR: Ribbed cellular type with pressure cap. Cooling system capacity. 16 qt. (17 with heater).

RADIATOR GRILLE: Chrome, lattice type (vertical and horizontal bars). Upper grille frame is integral with front edge of hood.

RADIATOR GRILLE GUARD: Accessory chrome horizontal bar between the two bumper guards.

RADIO: Choice of three accessory units: Signal-Seeking Radio—De luxe 8-tube (with rectifier) unit; has automatic tuner bar plus five pushbuttons set to predetermined stations. Pushbutton radio—De luxe 7-tube (with rectifier) unit; has five pushbuttons set to predetermined stations. Manual Tuning Radio—6-tube (with rectifier) unit. Controls and dial for each radio are mounted on center of instrument panel above glove compartment.

RADIO ANTENNA: Accessory telescoping nickel-chrome-brass antenna is mounted on right hand front fender.

RADIO SPEAKER: Quadrant-shaped speaker at right side of instrument panel. Accessory rear seat speaker (6″ x 9″) is mounted flush with parcel shelf; not available in station wagons and Convertible.

RAIN DEFLECTORS, SIDE WINDOW: Accessory chrome awnings installed above side windows; available in sets for 4-door and 2-door sedans and Club Coupe.

RAMP ANGLES: Angle of approach (front), 28°; angle of departure (rear), 16°.

REAR AXLE: Semi-floating type with hypoid drive gears, 2-pinion differential, flanged axle shafts, and single unit banjo-type housing with welded-on cover. Ratios—3.70 to 1 with Synchro-Mesh transmission. 4.11 to 1 with overdrive transmission, 3.55 to 1 with Powerglide automatic transmission.

REAR SUSPENSION: Longitudinal, chrome alloy steel, semi-elliptic leaf springs, 58″ long by 2″ wide; 4 leaves (5 in station wagons). Optional 6-leaf springs for heavy-duty service. Lubrication-eliminating leaf inserts. Outrigger mounting with compression shackles. Diagonally mounted, life-sealed, direct double-acting shock absorbers.

REARVIEW MIRROR: See Mirrors, Rearview.

REAR WINDOW: See Window, Rear.

RINGS: See Piston Rings.

RODS: See Connecting Rods.

ROOF BOW, CENTRAL: See Body Construction.

S

SAFETY GLASS: See Window Glass.

SCUFF PADS: Scuff-resistant vinyl panels at bottoms of doors and side walls and front seat; with chrome moldings in Bel Air models.

SEAT ADJUSTMENT, FRONT: 4.4″ total travel, on inclined plane (seat rises and tilts forward as it is moved ahead so driver sits in more erect position). Chrome pushbutton control at left side of seat riser.

Optional electric-power adjustment for Bel Air and "Two-Ten" sedans and coupes.

SEAT CONSTRUCTION: Full-width seats with S-wire springs on all-steel frames. Split center-folding front seat back rests in all 2-door models; centrally located, completely folding rear seat, in every station wagon, folds level with load platform. All seats comfortably cushioned; foam rubber cushions on front seats of all Bel Air and "Two-Ten" models and on rear seats of Bel Air sedans and coupes.

SEAT COVERS: See Seat Trim.

SEAT DIMENSIONS: Front — leg room, 43.1"; head room, 35.7"; hip room, 62.0"; shoulder room, 56.8". Rear—leg room, 40.8"; head room, 35.4"; hip room, 63.0"; shoulder room, 56.4". (These dimensions are for 4-door sedans. For other models, see Models section, pages 13-39.)

SEAT TRIM: Bel Air sedans—Combination of pattern cloth, gabardine flat cloth and vinyl. • Bel Air Sport Coupe and station wagon—Straw pattern cloth and vinyl • Bel Air Convertible—All vinyl. • "Two-Ten" sedans—Pattern cloth, ripple-weave gabardine and vinyl. • "Two-Ten" Club Coupe and station wagons — All vinyl. • "One-Fifty" sedans — Pattern cloth and vinyl. • "One-Fifty" station wagons—All vinyl. • Accessory sets of seat and back rest covers in plastic, nylon or fiber—in blue, brown or green—for 4-door and 2-door sedans. Accessory seat cushion covers of transparent nylon-dacron (6 colors) for 4-door and 2-door sedans and Sport Coupe.

SHAVER: Accessory 4-head electric shaver; plugs into cigarette lighter socket; operates either on 12 volts D.C. in car or on 110 volts A.C. in home.

SHOCK ABSORBERS: Permanently-lubricated, hydraulic, direct double-acting shock absorbers. Front shock absorbers mounted coaxially with coil springs; rear, mounted diagonally.

SPARK ADVANCE CONTROL: Dual automatic (centrifugal and vacuum).

SPARK PLUGS: 14-mm size, with neoprene caps for protection from moisture.

SPEEDOMETER: Located high and directly in front of driver. Equipped with odometer. Adjustable indirect lighting.

SPOT LIGHTS: Accessory combination of sealed beam spotlight and rearview mirror; mounted through body and controlled from inside car. Accessory portable sealed beam hand light with 12-foot cord; plugs into cigarette lighter socket.

SPRINGS: See Front and Rear Suspension.

STARTER: Solenoid-operated positive-shift starting motor. Key-turn control, combined with ignition lock switch; keyhole is lighted when car lights are on.

STEERING: Recirculating ball-nut steering gear; 20 to 1 ratio. Relay type linkage. Overall ratio, 25.7 to 1 (23.3 to 1 with power steering).

STEERING COLUMN: Concentric type, enclosing mechanism leading to transmission and direction signal control levers.

STEERING KNUCKLES: Self-adjusting spherical-joint steering knuckles with non-metallic bearing liners. Four lubrication fittings.

STEERING WHEEL: 18" diameter steel-reinforced plastic wheel (3-spoke in Bel Air models: 2-spoke in "Two-Ten" and "One-Fifty" models). Wheel hub emblem is gold-plated in Bel Air models; chrome-plated in others.

STOP LIGHTS: See Tail-and-Stop Lights.

STROKE: See Bore and Stroke.

SUN SHADES, INTERIOR: Two universally adjustable sliding sun shades in Bel Air (except Convertible) and "Two-Ten" models; one for driver in "One-Fifty" models. The two sun shades of the Convertible are hinged at both ends and swivel up or down. Accessory sun shade, for front-seat passenger, for "One-Fifty" models. In the sedans, the sun shades are covered with plain napped cloth with a vinyl hand hold; in other models, they are completely covered with vinyl.

SUN VISOR, OUTSIDE: Accessory metal visor painted to match car exterior and edged with chrome molding; available for all models except Convertible.

SUSPENSION: See Front Suspension and Rear Suspension.

SYNCHRO-MESH TRANSMISSION: See Transmission, Synchro-Mesh.

TAIL-AND-STOP LIGHTS: Two ruby-red, in tops of rear fender ends, provided with red reflex buttons. Chrome frames. Broad spacing of lights denotes car width in dark.

TAIL GATE, STATION WAGON: See Gate.

TAPPETS: See Valves.

TEMPERATURE INDICATOR, ENGINE: Bourdon-tube type with indirectly lighted dial on instrument panel.

TIMING CHAIN OR GEARS: Fabric composition and steel timing gears (6-cylinder engines); silent chain and sprocket drive (V8).

TIRES: 6.70-15-4 ply rating, extra-low-pressure tubeless tires; 24-pound inflation pressure (cold). Optional, 6 ply rating. Optional white walls (with black inner walls).

TISSUE DISPENSER: Accessory pivoting box, with chrome front; mounts below instrument panel; holds full standard size box of tissues.

TOP, TURRET: One-piece all-steel top reinforced by central roof bow and box-section side rails. Drip moldings at sides. Also see Convertible Top.

TRAFFIC LIGHT VIEWER: Accessory prism unit; mounts on top of instrument panel; shows traffic light in true colors when direct view of light is blocked.

TRANSMISSION, AUTOMATIC: Optional 3-element hydraulic torque converter, with planetary gears for reverse and automatic low. Selector lever on steering column. Lighted selector indicator (with P-N-D-L-R sequence) in instrument cluster. Safety switch in starter circuit. Oil cooler integrated with engine cooling system. Ratios: Maximum torque converter ratio, 2.10 to 1; planetary gear ratio, 1.82

to 1; maximum overall ratio, 3.82 to 1. Available with 136-hp Six, or V8.

TRANSMISSION, OVERDRIVE: Optional 3-pinion planetary-gear overdrive, combined with Synchro-Mesh transmission, provides an additional forward gear in which engine speed is reduced more than 22% for the same road speed as with conventional transmission. Gear ratio, .70 to 1. Accelerator control—electric cut-in by releasing accelerator treadle at approximately 30 mph; downshift to direct drive by pressing treadle to floor. Manual lockout handle, at right of steering column, is pulled all the way out to disengage overdrive.

TRANSMISSION, SYNCHRO-MESH: Heavy-duty 3-speed Synchro-Mesh transmission with gearshift lever on steering column. Gear ratios—first 2.94 to 1, second 1.68 to 1, third 1.00 to 1, reverse 2.94 to 1.

TREAD: Front tread, 58.0"; rear tread, 58.8".

TRIM: See Seat Trim.

TRUNK, SEDAN AND COUPE: Roomy trunk with extra-low sill; 20-cubic foot capacity (17-cubic-feet for Convertible). Rubber floor mat. Spare wheel-well at right with wheel inclined toward side-wall.

TRUNK LID, SEDAN AND COUPE: Double-walled deck lid with concealed, full-travel, torque-rod type counterbalancing hinges that cannot interfere with or damage luggage. Stationary chrome handle combined with plastic Chevrolet emblem. Weather-protected key lock below handle. Key release. Lid locks, without use of key, when slammed shut.

TRUNK LIGHT: Accessory light unit installs in trunk; lights automatically when lid is raised.

TURNING DIAMETER (Curb to Curb): 38 feet.

UNDERHOOD LIGHT: Accessory engine compartment light; lights automatically when hood is raised.

UNIVERSAL JOINTS: Two, with needle bearings.

UPHOLSTERY: See Interior Finishing Materials or Seat Trim.

VALVES: Silichrome steel valves (with special XCR alloy steel exhaust valves in 136-hp Six and V8). Close-grained cast iron valve guides pressed in cylinder head (6-cylinder engines); integral guides (V8). Variable pitch valve springs. Armasteel rocker arms operating on shafts (6-cylinder engines); special independent pressed steel rocker arms (V8). Mechanical valve tappets (self-adjusting, hydraulic valve lifters in engines with Powerglide automatic transmission).

VENTILATION, CAR: High-level air intake through five banks of louvers in top of cowl. Shroud-length plenum chamber in double-walled cowl; with water drainage to ground. Large outlet louvers in cowl sides direct air toward body level and toward floor. Pull-out knobs on instrument panel ends for individual control of two outlets. Air is heated to desired degree with use of accessory heater. Crank-operated side windows and ventipanes. Optional, compact single-unit all-weather air conditioner, by Frigidaire, for V8 models except Convertible.

VENTIPANES, NO-DRAFT: Crank-operated, pivoting, chrome-framed rectangular ventipanes (with sliding bolt locks) in front doors.

VINYL: Vinyl plastic on cloth backing; provides durable and washable, colorful material of pleasing design.

WATER JACKETS: Full-length jackets encircling each cylinder. Valve seats encircled by water passages, eliminating need for special inserts.

WATER PUMP: Self-adjusting, centrifugal type with permanently-lubricated double-row ball bearing, driven with engine fan by V-section belt.

WEIGHT, CAR: 3165 lb. shipping weight for "One-Fifty" 4-door sedan with 6-cylinder engine and Synchro-Mesh transmission. For other models, see Models section, pages 13-39.

WHEELBASE: 115" (59 per cent of car length).

WHEEL CARRIER: Accessory Continental-type carrier; mounts tire in cover outside trunk, allowing more trunk room.

WHEEL DISKS: Chrome full-size wheel disks on Bel Air models (chrome hub caps on others). Accessory for "Two-Ten" and "One-Fifty" models.

WHEEL RINGS: Accessory chrome wheel rings: for "Two-Ten" and "One-Fifty" models.

WHEELS: Short spoke steel disk wheels; 5" wide-base rims. Ball-type bearings.

WIDTH, CAR OVERALL: 74.0" (all models).

WINDOW GLASS: Safety glass. Safety plate glass in windshield, ventipanes, and rear window of every model (except rear window of Convertible, which is vinyl plastic) and in side windows of Bel Air Sport Coupe and Convertible. Total vision area, 24.4 sq. ft. in 4-door sedans (for other models, see Models section, pages 13-39.) Optional E-Z-Eye tinted safety plate glass in all windows, with or without shaded band on windshield.

WINDOW CONTROLS, SIDE: Crank type controls raise and lower all door windows, and rear-quarter windows of 2-door models except Utility Sedan and "One-Fifty" station wagons, which are stationary. Optional electric-power control for side windows of Bel Air and "Two-Ten" models; master control buttons for all four windows on driver's door; individual pushbutton at each window.

WINDOW, REAR: Single full-wraparound pane in all sedans and Sport and Club Coupes. Single curved pane in lift gate of station wagons. Zippered-in vinyl plastic rear window in Convertible top.

WINDOWS, REAR-QUARTER: 4-door sedans and Utility Sedan—Stationary panes. • 2-door sedans and Club Coupe – Crank-operated fully lowering panes. • Sport Coupe and Convertible—Crank-operated downward-swiveling panes. • 4-door station wagons—Stationary panes wrapped around rear corners of body. • "Two-Ten" 2-door station wagon—

Two panes per side with crank-operated lowering front pane and stationary wraparound rear pane. • "One-Fifty" 2-door station wagon—Two panes per side with stationary front pane and stationary wraparound rear pane.

WINDSHIELD: One-piece full-wraparound windshield with vertical pillars; vision area, 1018 sq. in. (975, Sport Coupe and Convertible). Full-width defrosting (with heater).

WINDSHIELD GLARE SHIELD: Accessory light-green plexiglass shield; mounts at top of windshield; filters out 80% of sun glare and bright lights.

WINDSHIELD WASHER: Accessory vacuum-operated washer controlled by pushbutton, or accessory foot-operated pressure type. Accessory unit automatically coordinates wiper and washer action.

WINDSHIELD WIPERS: Two vacuum-operated adjustable-speed wipers controlled by turn-knob at left of steering column. Accessory blades with rubber hoods for self-de-icing. Optional two-speed electric wipers.

WIRING JUNCTION BLOCK: Accessory unit placing fuses for all accessories in one location under instrument panel, at left of the steering column, for easy replacement.

Valve-in-Head Engine • Electric Starter • Polished Lacquer Finish • Headlight Dimmer Foot Switch • Harmonic Balancer • Finger-Tip Seat Adjustment • Stabilized Front End • No-Draft Ventipanes • Octane Selector • Flanged Rear Axle Shafts • Knee-Action • Complete Body Insulation • Turret Top • Box-Girder Frame • Unisteel Body • Diaphragm Spring Clutch • Bonded Brake Linings • "Hard-top" Sport Coupe • Automatic Transmission • Power Steering • Power Brakes • Automatic Seat and Window Controls • Wraparound Windshield • High-Level Ventilation • Out-Rigger Rear Suspension • Air Conditioner • 12-Volt Electrical System • Ball-Race Steering • Braking Dive Control

*Features introduced by Chevrolet before both Ford and Plymouth.

COMPETITION

It's just good business to sell cars on their merits alone. But it may become necessary for Chevrolet salesmen to make comparisons of the Motoramic Chevrolet with competitive cars to answer customers' questions more effectively. Based on studies of competitive cars and published specifications and literature concerning them, this section of the book points out:

- Chevrolet's superiorities over Ford.

- Chevrolet's superiorities over Plymouth.

- Chevrolet's superiorities over BOTH.

CHEVROLET VS FORD

Chevrolet Superiorities

MORE COMPACT SIZE. Overhang is the length between the bumper and wheel center at each end of the car. Although CHEVROLET and FORD wheelbases are practically the same (115" and 115.5"), CHEVROLET'S overhang is nearly three inches less than FORD'S, making car handling and parking easier. Similarly, although the CHEVROLET is wider inside, the FORD is bulkier with an outside width of 76 inches, two inches more than CHEVROLET.

STEEPER RAMP ANGLES. CHEVROLET'S angle of approach is 28°; FORD'S is only 23°. CHEVROLET'S angle of departure is 16°; FORD'S is only 14°.

SMALLER TURNING CIRCLE. The CHEVROLET can make a complete turn in a street only 38 feet wide. The street would have to be widened three feet before the FORD could make the same turn.

BROADER REAR TREAD. For greater riding stability, CHEVROLET'S rear tread is 58.8", nearly three inches more than FORD'S 56" rear tread.

LOWER CAR HEIGHT. CHEVROLET'S loaded height is 60½ inches, ½ inch less than the FORD, for better appearance.

MORE HEAD ROOM. Although the FORD height is greater, the CHEVROLET'S average head room is nearly one inch more than the FORD'S: 35.7" vs 35.1" in the front seat and 35.4" vs 34.2" in the rear seat.

MORE HIP ROOM. Although the FORD is broader outside (76" vs 74"), the CHEVROLET is broader *inside* with a 1½" wider front seat (hip room: 62.0" vs 60.5") and a rear seat that is nearly three inches wider (hip room: 63.0" vs 60.3").

MORE ENTRANCE ROOM. CHEVROLET'S front-door entrance room measures 29.4"; FORD'S is 29.2". CHEVROLET'S rear-door entrance room is two inches greater than FORD'S: 28.1" compared to 26.2".

GREATER VISION AREA. CHEVROLET provides 3515 sq. in. in glass area, 166 more than FORD'S 3349 sq. in.

TALLER WINDSHIELD. With nearly one inch more height than FORD (17.5" vs 16.7"), CHEVROLET'S windshield provides greater vision of overhead traffic lights.

LARGER SIDE WINDOWS. CHEVROLET'S total side window area is 1429 sq. in.; FORD'S is only 1221 sq. in.

LARGER REAR WINDOW. CHEVROLET'S rear window area is 1067 sq. in.; FORD'S is only 1030 sq. in.

HEAVIER BASIC CAR. CHEVROLET'S lowest-priced conventional "six" weighs 60 pounds more than the comparable FORD (3165 lb. vs 3105 lb.).

BETTER WEIGHT DISTRIBUTION: When the V8 engine and automatic transmission are provided, the weight of the CHEVROLET is increased only 65 pounds. Excessive dead weight, however, boosts the FORD car weight by 215 pounds when their V8 and automatic transmission are installed. (It's like carrying an extra passenger all the time.) As the result, the FORD front wheels must carry 205 pounds more weight than those of the CHEVROLET (1990 lb. vs 1785 lb.), making steering and handling harder. To carry this extra dead weight FORD'S recommended tire pressures are 26 pounds for the front tires and only 23 for the rear. CHEVROLET'S recommended tire pressure is 24 pounds for every tire—for softer, smoother riding and more stable handling.

LESS WORK PER HORSEPOWER. No matter what kind of power team is used, FORD engines must pull more weight per horsepower than CHEVROLET engines, as shown in the chart at the top of the next page. As the result, CHEVROLET engines perform better and operate with greater economy.

POUNDS PER HORSEPOWER

TRANSMISSION	6-CYL. ENGINE		V8 ENGINE	
	Chevrolet	Ford	Chevrolet	Ford
Automatic	24.0	26.7	20.0	20.4
Overdrive	26.0	26.2	19.6	20.1
Conventional	25.7	25.9	19.4	19.9

LOWER INITIAL COST: Model-for-model, FORDS cost $13 to $31 more to buy than CHEVROLETS *(advertised delivered prices).*

STYLE — APPEARANCE

Chevrolet Superiorities

COMPLETELY NEW BODY. CHEVROLET'S body is completely new in size, structure, and styling. FORD'S body resembles that of last year.

INTEGRAL HEADLIGHT HOODS. CHEVROLET'S handsome headlight hoods are smoothly formed in the graceful front fenders—without any disturbing break in the painted surface. FORD'S protruding hoods are formed in the headlight rims, with unsightly breaks where the rims clamp on the fenders.

DIP-DOWN BELT LINE. CHEVROLET'S distinctive "dip-down" belt line is just one of many styling notes that make CHEVROLET a truly modern car. FORD'S conservative belt line is high and straight.

SEPARATE REAR-QUARTER WINDOWS IN SEDANS. CHEVROLET provides the modern vision and style advantages of separate rear-quarter windows in all four-door sedans. FORD four-door sedans do not have this feature.

WRAPAROUND REAR-QUARTER WINDOWS IN STATION WAGONS. Rear-quarter windows that curve gracefully around the rear corners of the body are distinctive style and visibility features of CHEV-

ROLET station wagons. The rear-quarter windows of FORD station wagons are flat glass.

POLISHED LAQUER FINISH. The same high quality lacquer that is used on the finest cars gives the CHEVROLET a deep, long-lasting luster—a luster that is not possible with FORD'S synthetic enamel finish.

QUALITY — COMFORT — CONVENIENCE

Chevrolet Superiorities

BODY-BY-FISHER QUALITY. Body-by-Fisher quality, comfort, and convenience are found only in CHEV-ROLET in the low-price field.

FIRM, SOLID DOOR HANDLES. CHEVROLET'S outside door handles are solid castings that assure a smooth firm grip. FORD'S handles are cast with a hollow on the inner side.

SINGLE CAR KEY. There is no need to select a key when opening CHEVROLET locks, because one key operates all locks in the car. With a FORD, two keys are required: one for the ignition and door locks, one for the glove and luggage compartment locks.

UNLOCKED "OFF" IN IGNITION-STARTER. An unlocked "OFF" position in the ignition-starter switch permits the CHEVROLET driver to leave his car in a parking lot in an operable condition, yet he still may take the key with him knowing that the contents of his locked glove compartment and trunk are safe. The FORD owner must leave his ignition and door lock key with the car.

AUTOMATIC LOCK WEATHER SHIELDS. The shields that seal CHEVROLET outside locks from the weather automatically uncover or cover the key-hole when the key is inserted or removed. FORD lock weather shields must be pushed aside before the key can be inserted.

KEYLESS DOOR LOCKING. The CHEVROLET may be conveniently locked from outside without use of the key. It is still necessary to hand lock the FORD with a key.

CLEARLY-VISIBLE AUTOMATIC-TRANSMISSION SELECTOR QUADRANT. CHEVROLET'S quadrant is clustered with the speedometer high on the instrument panel. FORD'S is near the base of the steering column.

"LOW" AND "REVERSE" SIDE-BY-SIDE. CHEVROLET'S automatic transmission selector sequence places "low" and "reverse" side-by-side for easier rocking out of sand or snow. In the FORDOMATIC sequence, "low" and "reverse" are separated by "neutral" and "drive."

"PARK" OR "NEUTRAL" STARTS. It is not necessary, as in the FORD, to shift the CHEVROLET automatic transmission selector from "park" to "neutral" before starting the car. CHEVROLET starts can be made in either "park" or "neutral."

AUTOMATIC CHOKE. CHEVROLET'S automatic choke provides quick, dependable starting at all engine temperatures. FORD still uses a hand-operated choke.

POSITIVE-SHIFT STARTER. CHEVROLET'S starter assures positive starts without gear clashing and chipping of gear teeth. FORD'S anti-kickout starting motor drive can cause severe gear clashing and chipping of gear teeth.

FOUR-DOOR AUTOMATIC INTERIOR-LIGHT SWITCHES. In addition to automatic switches at both front doors of all Bel Air and "Two-Ten" models, CHEVROLET provides automatic switches at both rear doors of Bel Air four-door models. FORD has only front door switches in its Fairlane and Customline series.

INTERIOR-LIGHT CONTROL BY MAIN LIGHT SWITCH. CHEVROLET'S hand control of the interior light is in easy reach of the driver's left hand. FORD'S hand control is in the ceiling integral with the dome light.

CENTRAL GLOVE COMPARTMENT. CHEVRO-
LET'S glove compartment is in easy reach of both
the driver and front seat passenger. FORD'S glove
compartment is located at the extreme right of the
instrument panel.

AUTOMATIC GLOVE COMPARTMENT LIGHT.
CHEVROLET provides this convenience feature as
standard equipment in all Bel Air and "Two-Ten"
models. FORD provides it only as an accessory at
extra cost.

ELECTRIC CLOCK. An electric clock is regular
equipment in every CHEVROLET Bel Air. FORD
provides a stem-wind clock in its comparable Fairlane series.

FULLY-ADJUSTABLE SUN SHADES. In addition
to being adjustable up and down and from front to
side, CHEVROLET sun shades (except in the Convertible) slide on their shafts to provide fullest protection from sun glare. FORD sun shades do not
slide.

ELECTRIC WINDSHIELD WIPERS. In addition to
its efficient standard windshield wipers, CHEVRO-
LET provides, as accessories, electric wipers that
maintain a constant speed regardless of engine load.
FORD still offers only a vacuum pump (at extra
cost) to help remedy slow wiper operation under extreme engine load conditions.

CONCENTRIC STEERING COLUMN. As in the most
expensive cars, smartness is added to the CHEV-
ROLET interior by enclosing all mechanisms within
the steering column. FORD'S gearshift mechanism is
exposed to view.

CRANK-REGULATED VENTIPANES. A convenience found only in CHEVROLET and higher-
priced cars, the handy easy-acting crank regulators
hold the CHEVROLET ventipanes in any position.
FORD'S smaller ventipanes have no regulators; are
held open by friction only.

HIGH-LEVEL AIR INTAKE. CHEVROLET'S
modern air intake that spans the cowl just ahead of
the windshield, as on higher-priced cars, receives

cooler, cleaner air than FORD's intakes, which are located low in front of the car.

FRIGIDAIRE AIR CONDITIONER. Only CHEVROLET in its field provides as optional equipment, Frigidaire's compact, single-unit air conditioner. With this air conditioner, all the main mechanical components are located in the engine compartment instead of taking up trunk space as do other types.

EXTRA-LOW-SILL TRUNK. CHEVROLET'S trunk sill is only one inch above the trunk floor. Everything put in FORD'S trunk must be lifted over an 8½-inch high sill.

STRUCTURE

Chevrolet Superiorities

CENTER ROOF BOW. Every CHEVROLET steel top is strengthened by a rigid steel roof bow. And, in all sedan-type models and station wagons, this roof bow combines with the door pillars and an underbody cross beam to complete a sturdy body mid-section frame. FORD sedans and station wagons lack this safety feature.

DOUBLE-WALLED COWL. Two cowls in one unit provide greater strength and rigidity in every CHEVROLET body. The FORD body does not have this safety feature.

WELDED-IN INSTRUMENT PANEL. CHEVROLET'S instrument panel is welded into the cowl structure and serves as an integral structural member of the body. FORD'S instrument panel is just bolted in place.

FULL DOUBLE-WALLED BODY SIDES. CHEVROLET body sides including the cowl, doors, rear-quarter and trunk sides, are double-walled from front to rear for greatest durability and safety. Moreover, the sides of the basic body are built as units to assure better door fits. No other low-priced car has this combination of structural features.

MECHANICALLY-ATTACHED DOOR SEALS. In addition to retention by rubber cement, the rubber seals of CHEVROLET doors are retained by many metal clips. FORD'S door seals, retained only by cement, may loosen and dangle.

COWL-REINFORCED CHASSIS FRAME. CHEV-ROLET utilizes the great strength of its arch-like, double-walled cowl to reinforce the chassis frame at its center. This permits the frame to be made lighter in weight with a gain of 50 per cent in rigidity. Be-cause FORD'S frame requires five cross members and a K-brace to provide the necessary structural rigidity, extra dead weight, that must be pulled by the engine, is added to the car.

RIDE

Chevrolet Superiorities

SEALED, PLASTIC-LINED FRONT SUSPENSION JOINTS. Unlike the metallic bearings in FORD'S front suspension joints, CHEVROLET'S spherical joints have sealed linings of a special plastic that has exceptional resistance to wear and low friction quali-ties that contribute to smooth, easy steering.

LONGER REAR SPRINGS. CHEVROLET'S extra-long (58") springs provide superior riding smooth-ness. FORD'S rear springs are five inches shorter (53") and require an extra spring leaf to assure satisfactory riding comfort.

WIDER-SPACED REAR SPRINGS. Not only is CHEVROLET'S rear tread nearly three inches greater than FORD'S, but CHEVROLET'S rear springs are four inches farther apart than FORD'S—contributing further to CHEVROLET'S superior riding comfort and stability. This is the result of CHEVROLET'S out-rigger rear suspension in which the springs are mounted outside the side rails. In FORD'S design, the springs are mounted underneath the side rails.

LIVE-RUBBER BODY MOUNTINGS. Molded live-rubber cushions, strategically located, isolate CHEVROLET'S body from the transmission of road sensations through the chassis frame. FORD'S body is rigidly mounted to the frame on wafer-thin shims.

ENGINE (Both V8's and Sixes)

Chevrolet Superiorities

FORGED STEEL CRANKSHAFT. CHEVROLET'S rigid steel crankshaft contributes greatly to smooth engine operation and superior engine durability. FORD uses a cast iron crankshaft.

LOCKED-IN-ROD PISTON PINS. CHEVROLET'S piston pins, solidly held in the connecting rod ends, prevent deflections of the upper ends of the connecting rods—thereby contributing to quieter engine operation and to greater engine durability. FORD'S "floating type" piston pins tend to permit such deflections.

HYDRAULIC VALVE LIFTERS. CHEVROLET'S self-adjusting hydraulic valve lifters (used in Power-glide models) provide quieter, smoother valve operation than FORD'S conventional mechanical valve lifters.

PULSATOR-TYPE FUEL PUMP. CHEVROLET'S pulsator-type fuel pump makes possible a more constant supply of gasoline at all times. FORD does not have this feature.

GASOLINE FILTER IN FUEL TANK. CHEVROLET'S filter prevents water from getting into the gasoline line. FORD'S filter is in the fuel pump and does not prevent water from entering and freezing in the gasoline line in cold weather.

FLOATING OIL INTAKE. CHEVROLET'S oil intake, floating near the top of the oil in the crankcase, provides sediment-free oil at all times. FORD's oil pump is stationary near the bottom of the oil pan and can pick up harmful sediment.

FOUR-BLADE ENGINE FAN. CHEVROLET'S fan provides smoother, quieter, and more efficient air circulation than FORD'S three-blade fan, which must run faster and consequently is noisier.

12-VOLT ELECTRICAL SYSTEM. CHEVROLET'S 12-volt system assures greater capacity, more efficient battery charging, and a finer high speed performance. Even with its greatly increased power accessory drain, FORD still uses a 6-volt system which can bring an unusual drain on the battery and cause an electrical breakdown.

54-PLATE BATTERY. CHEVROLET'S 54-plate battery provides constant, sure-fire energy to power the many electrical conveniences which have been added to modern cars. Even though FORD has added power accessories, FORD still retains its conventional 51-plate battery.

DUAL AUTOMATIC SPARK ADVANCE CONTROL. CHEVROLET'S automatic centrifugal and vacuum spark advance control provides sure and precise timing at all engine speeds. FORD'S full-vacuum spark advance control tends to break down at varying engine speeds.

FOUR-POINT ENGINE MOUNTING. Four rubber mountings, two at the front and two at the rear of CHEVROLET engines, not only smother engine vibrations but also reduce engine torque reactions in the frame and body to the minimum. To support the weight of its engines, FORD uses two mountings at the front but only one at the rear.

V8 EXTRAS

Chevrolet Superiorities

SHORTER STROKE DESIGN. CHEVROLET'S large bore (3.75") and short stroke (3.0") provide a better oversquare design than FORD'S smaller bore (3.62") and longer stroke (3.30")—resulting in up to 14 per cent less travel per mile for each piston and longer engine life.

LESS ENGINE WEIGHT. CHEVROLET'S compact and sturdy V8 engine weighs only 488 pounds, whereas FORD'S V8 weighs 586 pounds—98 more pounds that must be pulled.

HIGHER COMPRESSION RATIO. CHEVROLET'S 8.0 to 1 compression ratio provides better performance and gasoline economy than FORD'S standard ratio of 7.6 to 1.

INDEPENDENT VALVE MECHANISMS. CHEVROLET'S exclusive separate valve train linkage provides quieter, more positive valve action at all speeds than FORD'S conventional linkage.

SMALLER OIL REQUIREMENTS. The CHEVROLET V8 requires one quart less oil every oil change than the FORD V8. The respective oil refill capacities are four quarts and five quarts.

PARALLEL-FLOW PRESSURE COOLING. CHEVROLET'S V8 cooling system provides independent cooling for each bank of four cylinders—thereby providing more even coolant distribution for all cylinders. With FORD'S "series flow" cooling system, the coolant must flow through one bank of cylinders before it enters the second bank.

"SIX" EXTRAS

Chevrolet Superiorities

CHOICE OF *TWO* SIXES. CHEVROLET offers a choice of two six-cylinder engines: the "Blue-Flame 123" and the "Blue-Flame 136." FORD provides one six.

GREATER POWER IN *BOTH* SIXES. The CHEVROLET "Blue-Flame 123," used with Synchro-Mesh and Overdrive transmissions, is rated at 123 horsepower. The CHEVROLET "Blue-Flame 136," used with the automatic transmission, provides 136 horsepower. FORD'S one six develops 120 horsepower, regardless of transmission choice.

GREATER TORQUE IN *BOTH* SIXES. Both CHEVROLET sixes provide better acceleration and hill-climbing ability because of their higher torque ratings: 209 ft. lb. at 2200 rpm. for the "Blue-Flame 136" and 207 at 2000 for the "Blue-Flame 123." FORD'S one six is rated at only 195 ft. lb.—at the higher engine speed of 2400 rpm.

CONCENTRIC CARBURETOR. The concentric carburetor that is used on both CHEVROLET sixes has twin floats that maintain a balanced fuel mixture even on curves or grades. The FORD Six carburetor does not have this feature.

TRANSMISSIONS – STEERING – BRAKES

Chevrolet Superiorities

DIAPHRAGM SPRING CLUTCH. CHEVROLET'S simple diaphragm spring clutch always provides full facing contact, and the light pedal pressure required for its disengagement actually decreases as the pedal is pushed down. FORD'S clutch, with its many coil springs, is a more complicated mechanism and requires increased pedal pressure as the engine speed increases.

WATER COOLING OF AUTOMATIC-TRANSMISSION OIL. FORD'S automatic transmission still uses air cooling as compared to CHEVROLET'S more efficient, controlled water cooling.

LEAKPROOF REAR AXLE. CHEVROLET'S new design and installation of rear wheel bearing seals make the rear axle practically leakproof. FORD'S method of installing their seals is the same that CHEVROLET discarded last year.

RECIRCULATING BALL-NUT STEERING GEAR. As in the most expensive cars, recirculating ball bearings in CHEVROLET'S steering gear reduce friction to the minimum to make steering smoother and easier and to make the steering gear more durable. FORD still uses a worm and roller steering gear in its standard steering system.

BONDED BRAKE LININGS. CHEVROLET'S brake linings are bonded to the brake shoes to make braking smoother and to double the life of the linings. FORD'S riveted brake linings require replacement when they wear down to the rivets.

BRAKING DIVE CONTROL. CHEVROLET'S braking dive control greatly reduces nose-diving of the car under all stopping conditions, assuring more comfortable stops and lessening the possibility of bumper locking and front end damage in case of sudden stops in close quarters. This feature is exclusive to CHEVROLET—in the industry.

CHEVROLET VS PLYMOUTH

Chevrolet Superiorities

MORE COMPACT LENGTH. Overhang is the length between the bumper and wheel center at each end of the car. Although CHEVROLET and PLYMOUTH wheelbases are the same (115″), CHEVROLET'S overhang is eight inches less than PLYMOUTH'S, making car handling and parking easier.

STEEPER RAMP ANGLES. CHEVROLET'S angle of approach is 28°; PLYMOUTH'S is only 22°. CHEVROLET'S angle of departure is 16°; PLYMOUTH'S is only 12°.

SMALLER TURNING CIRCLE. The CHEVROLET can make a complete turn in a street only 38 feet wide. The street would have to be widened two feet before the PLYMOUTH could make the same turn.

MORE ENTRANCE ROOM. CHEVROLET provides about ½″ more front-door entrance room (29.4″ vs 29.0″) and nearly one-inch more rear-door entrance room (28.1″ vs 27.3″) than PLYMOUTH.

MORE HEAD ROOM. CHEVROLET'S front-seat head room measures 35.7″; PLYMOUTH'S is 35.0″. CHEVROLET'S rear-seat head room is 35.4″ whereas PLYMOUTH'S is only 34.6″, almost one inch less.

GREATER VISION AREA. CHEVROLET provides 3515 sq. in. in glass area, 127 more than PLYMOUTH'S 3388 sq. in.

TALLER WINDSHIELD. With one inch more height than PLYMOUTH (17.5″ vs 16.5″), CHEVROLET'S windshield provides a better view of overhead traffic lights.

HEAVIER BASIC CAR. CHEVROLET'S lowest-priced conventional "six" weighs 35 pounds more than the comparable PLYMOUTH (3165 lb. vs 3130 lb.).

BETTER WEIGHT DISTRIBUTION. When the V8 engine and automatic transmission are provided, the weight of the CHEVROLET is increased only 65 pounds. Excessive dead weight, however, boosts the PLYMOUTH car weight by 190 pounds when their V8 and automatic transmission are installed. (It's like carrying an extra passenger all the time.) As the result, the PLYMOUTH front wheels must carry 165 more pounds than those of the CHEVROLET (1950 lb. vs 1785 lb.), making steering and handling harder. To carry this extra dead weight, PLYMOUTH recommends a tire pressure of 26 pounds for cars with V8 engines, although they recommend a pressure of 24 pounds for their cars with six-cylinder engines. CHEVROLET'S recommended pressure is 24 pounds for every tire, whether the engine is a V8 or six— for softer, smoother riding, and easier handling.

LESS WEIGHT PER HORSEPOWER. No matter what kind of power team is used, the PLYMOUTH Six must pull more weight per horsepower than the CHEVROLET Sixes. And, even though PLYMOUTH'S V8 engine is rated at 167-hp in comparison with CHEVROLET'S 162-hp, the two engines pull almost the same weights per horsepower, as shown in the following chart:

POUNDS PER HORSEPOWER

TRANSMISSION	6-CYL. ENGINE		V8 ENGINE	
	Chevrolet	Plymouth	Chevrolet	Plymouth
Automatic	24.0	27.4	20.0	19.9
Overdrive	26.0	27.0	19.6	19.6
Conventional	25.7	26.8	19.4	19.5

LARGER BRAKES. CHEVROLET'S Jumbo Drum Brakes are eleven inches in diameter for every wheel. PLYMOUTH wheel brakes are ten inches in diameter, except PLYMOUTH V8's, which have 11-inch brakes for the front wheels and 10-inch brakes for the rear wheels.

LOWER INITIAL COST. Model-for-model, PLYM-OUTHS cost $46 to $66 more to buy than CHEV-ROLETS *(advertised delivered prices).*

MODELS — STYLE — APPEARANCE

Chevrolet Superiorities

WIDER MODEL CHOICE: CHEVROLET offers 14 models (15, with Nomad) in three *complete* lines. PLYMOUTH offers twelve; with a choice of only two- and four-door sedans in their Savoy line.

DIP-DOWN BELT LINE. CHEVROLET'S distinctive "dip-down" belt line is only one of the many features that label CHEVROLET the style leader in its field. PLYMOUTH'S conservative belt line is high and straight.

SEPARATE REAR-QUARTER WINDOWS IN SEDANS. CHEVROLET provides separate rear-quarter windows in all four-door sedans. PLYM-OUTH four-door sedans do not have this modern styling and visibility feature.

WRAPAROUND REAR-QUARTER WINDOWS IN STATION WAGONS. Rear-quarter windows that curve gracefully around the rear corners of the body are distinctive style and visibility features of CHEV-ROLET station wagons. The rear-quarter windows of PLYMOUTH station wagons are flat glass.

FOUR-FENDER VISIBILITY. CHEVROLET'S grace-ful fenders are all clearly visible from the driver's seat to serve as guides in maneuvering the car. Only the front fenders of the PLYMOUTH are visible to the seated driver.

CONTOURED WRAPAROUND BUMPERS. CHEV-ROLET bumpers are shaped to the contour of the front and rear ends of the car and are provided with anti-lock type bumper guards. PLYMOUTH bumpers are plain, and PLYMOUTH bumper guards do not have the anti-lock feature.

POLISHED LACQUER FINISH. The same high quality lacquer that is used on the finest cars gives the CHEVROLET a deep long-lasting luster—a luster that is not possible with PLYMOUTH'S synthetic enamel finish.

QUALITY — COMFORT — CONVENIENCE

Chevrolet Superiorities

BODY-BY-FISHER QUALITY. Body-by-Fisher quality, comfort, and convenience are found only in CHEVROLET in the low-price field.

FIRM, SOLID DOOR HANDLES. CHEVROLET'S outside door handles are solid castings that assure a smooth firm grip. PLYMOUTH'S handles are cast with a hollow on the inner side.

SINGLE CAR KEY. There is no need to select a key when opening CHEVROLET locks, because one key operates all locks in the car. With a PLYMOUTH, two keys are required: one for the ignition and door locks, one for the glove and luggage compartment locks.

AUTOMATIC LOCK WEATHER SHIELDS. The shields that seal CHEVROLET outside locks from the weather automatically uncover or cover the keyhole when the key is inserted or removed. PLYMOUTH lock weather shields must be pushed aside before the key can be inserted.

KEYLESS DOOR LOCKING. With button-on-sill locks inside every door, the CHEVROLET may be conveniently locked from outside without use of the key. It is still necessary to hand-lock the PLYMOUTH from outside with a key.

FOUR-DOOR AUTOMATIC INTERIOR-LIGHT SWITCHES. In addition to automatic switches at both front doors of all Bel Air and "Two-Ten" models, CHEVROLET provides automatic switches at both rear doors of Bel Air four-door models. PLYMOUTH provides just one automatic switch— at its right side front door in Belvedere and Savoy models.

INTERIOR-LIGHT CONTROL BY MAIN LIGHT SWITCH. CHEVROLET'S hand control of the interior light is on the instrument panel within easy reach of the driver's left hand. PLYMOUTH'S hand control is in the ceiling integral with the dome light.

MORE CONVENIENT INSTRUMENT PANEL. On CHEVROLET'S instrument panel, all instruments are in a single cluster . . . and the cluster and all hand controls are located directly in front of the driver. On PLYMOUTH'S instrument panel, the instruments are all separate dials and both the battery charge indicator and the water temperature indicator are located to the right, out of the driver's range of vision.

RED BATTERY CHARGE AND OIL PRESSURE WARNING LIGHTS. These modern indicators are located on the CHEVROLET speedometer quadrant and flash only when the oil pressure is low or the battery is not charging. PLYMOUTH still uses dials.

CIGARETTE LIGHTER. In all CHEVROLET Bel Air and "Two-Ten" models, the cigarette lighter is standard equipment. (A feature of this lighter is the guard around the element to catch burning tobacco fragments so they won't burn clothing.) The PLYM-OUTH cigarette lighter is available only at extra cost.

ELECTRIC CLOCK. A handsome electric clock, built neatly into the instrument panel, is standard equipment in CHEVROLET Bel Air models and is available at extra cost in other CHEVROLETS. The PLYMOUTH clock is available only at extra cost in all models.

POSITIVE-SHIFT STARTER. CHEVROLET'S key-turn ignition-starter switch is clearly labelled with all key positions, and CHEVROLET's starter provides positive starts without gear clashing and chipping of gear teeth. PLYMOUTH'S ignition-starter switch is unlabelled, and PLYMOUTH'S anti-kickout starting motor can cause severe gear clashing and chipping of gear teeth.

UNLOCKED "OFF" IN IGNITION-STARTER SWITCH. This position in the ignition-starter switch permits the CHEVROLET driver to leave his car in a parking lot in an operatable condition, yet he still may take his key with him knowing that the contents of his locked glove compartment and trunk are safe. PLYMOUTH drivers must leave the ignition and door lock key with their cars.

LIGHTED AUTOMATIC-TRANSMISSION QUAD-RANT. The handy control lever of CHEVROLET'S automatic transmission is located below the steering wheel . . . and changes in position selections are clearly shown on the large selector quadrant which is built into and lighted with the instrument cluster. PLYMOUTH'S automatic-transmission selector lever slot on the instrument panel is unlighted.

"PARK" POSITION IN AUTOMATIC-TRANSMIS-SION QUADRANT. A simple shift of the transmission selector lever operates a parking lock that makes the CHEVROLET push-proof. The standard parking brake pull-handle is the only parking control of the PLYMOUTH.

BETTER-EQUIPPED GLOVE COMPARTMENT. The door of CHEVROLET'S glove compartment is equipped with a key lock and opens level to form a handy shelf. And, in Bel Air and "Two-Ten" models, the compartment is equipped with an automatic light. The PLYMOUTH glove compartment door hangs down when opened, and both lock and light are available only at extra cost.

CONCENTRIC STEERING COLUMN IN ALL MODELS. Smartness is added to every CHEVRO-LET interior by enclosing, within the steering column, the mechanisms leading to the transmission and direction signal controls. PLYMOUTH'S standard gearshift mechanism is on the steering column and is exposed to view.

CRANK-REGULATED VENTIPANES. A convenience found only in CHEVROLET and higher-priced cars, the handy easy-acting crank regulators hold the CHEVROLET ventipanes in any position. PLYM-OUTH ventipanes have no regulators; are held open by friction only.

WIDE HIGH-LEVEL AIR INTAKE. CHEVROLET'S modern air intake that spans the cowl just ahead of the windshield provides controlled ventilation to the car interior. PLYMOUTH still uses a small cowl ventilator.

FRIGIDAIRE AIR CONDITIONER. Only CHEVROLET in its field provides, as optional equipment, Frigidaire's compact, single-unit air conditioner. With this air conditioner, all the main mechanical components are located in the engine compartment. PLYMOUTH'S Airtemp air conditioner requires useful trunk space for its installation.

S-WIRE SEAT SPRINGS. CHEVROLET seat springs are of the modern sinuated S-wire construction that assures uniform resilient sitting comfort and provides space under the front seat for the circulation of air to the rear seat. PLYMOUTH seat springs are built up of many individual coils that take up space below the front seat.

FOAM-RUBBER SEAT CUSHIONS. Foam-rubber seat cushions are standard equipment in all CHEVROLET Bel Air seats and in CHEVROLET "Two-Ten" front seats. PLYMOUTH charges extra for foam-rubber cushions in any model.

CENTER-FOLD FRONT-SEAT BACK RESTS. In CHEVROLET two-door models, the front-seat back rest is divided at the center, providing more entrance room to the rear seat than is possible with PLYMOUTH'S 1/3-2/3 split front-seat back rest.

EXTRA-LOW-SILL TRUNK. CHEVROLET'S trunk sill is only one inch above the floor. Everything put in PLYMOUTH'S trunk must be lifted over a 7½-inch high sill.

KEY-RELEASE SLAM-LOCK TRUNK. CHEVROLET'S trunk lid is ready to open with a simple turn of a key, and is automatically locked when closed. PLYMOUTH'S trunk lid requires a key turn and a press of a pushbutton to be ready to open, and must be locked with a key.

LINOLEUM-SURFACED STATION WAGON LOAD COMPARTMENT FLOOR. The load compartment floor, tailgate, and the surface of the folded rear seat in every CHEVROLET station wagon are covered with durable, ribbed linoleum. A loose rubber mat covers the floor of PLYMOUTH station wagons.

STRUCTURE

Chevrolet Superiorities

CENTER ROOF BOW. Every CHEVROLET steel top is strengthened by a rigid steel roof bow. And, in all sedan-type models and station wagons, this roof bow combines with the door pillars and an underbody cross beam to complete a sturdy body midsection frame. PLYMOUTH does not have this safety feature.

DOUBLE-WALLED COWL. Two cowls in one unit provide greater strength and rigidity at the front of every CHEVROLET body. The PLYMOUTH body does not have this safety feature.

WELDED-IN INSTRUMENT PANEL. CHEVROLET'S instrument panel is welded into the cowl structure and serves as an integral structural member of the body. PLYMOUTH'S instrument panel is merely bolted in place.

FULL DOUBLE-WALLED BODY SIDES. CHEVROLET body sides including the cowl, doors, rear-quarter and trunk sides, are double-walled from front to rear for greatest durability and safety. Moreover, the sides of the basic body are built as units to assure better door fits. No other low-priced car has this combination of structural features.

MECHANICALLY-ATTACHED DOOR SEALS. In addition to retention by rubber cement, the rubber seals of CHEVROLET doors are retained by many metal clips. PLYMOUTH'S door seals, retained only by cement, may loosen and dangle.

COWL-REINFORCED CHASSIS FRAME. CHEVROLET utilizes the great strength of its arch-like double-walled cowl to reinforce the chassis frame at its center. This permits the frame to be made lighter in weight with a gain of 50 per cent in rigidity. Because PLYMOUTH'S frame requires four cross members to provide the necessary structural rigidity; extra dead weight than must be pulled by the engine is added to the car.

RIDE

Chevrolet Superiorities

SPHERICAL JOINT FRONT SUSPENSION. CHEVROLET'S independent front suspension system employs unique sealed spherical outer joints that also serve as steering knuckle bearings. The linings of these joints are a special plastic that has exceptional resistance to wear and low friction qualities. As the result, the action of the coil springs is easier for greater riding comfort, steering is easier, and durability is increased—and only four lubrication points are required. PLYMOUTH'S front suspension employs conventional metal outer end bearings and separate steering knuckle bushings—and has 16 points that must be lubricated.

LONGER REAR SPRINGS. CHEVROLET'S extra-long (58") rear springs provide superior riding smoothness. PLYMOUTH'S rear springs are one-half foot shorter: 52".

OUTRIGGER REAR SUSPENSION. CHEVROLET'S extra-long rear springs are mounted parallel, outside the frame side members, four inches farther apart than PLYMOUTH'S angle-mounted springs, for greater riding stability.

ENGINE
(Both V8's and Sixes)

Chevrolet Superiorities

12-VOLT ELECTRICAL SYSTEM. CHEVROLET'S 12-volt system assures greater capacity, more efficient battery charging, and a finer high speed performance. Even with its greatly increased power accessory drain, PLYMOUTH still uses a 6-volt system which can bring an unusual drain on the battery and cause an electrical breakdown.

54-PLATE BATTERY. CHEVROLET'S 54-plate battery provides constant, sure-fire energy to power the many electrical conveniences which have been added to modern cars. Even though PLYMOUTH offers optional power accessories, PLYMOUTH retains its conventional 45-plate battery.

FOUR-POINT ENGINE MOUNTING. Four rubber mountings, two at the front and two at the rear of CHEVROLET engines, not only smother engine vibrations but also reduce engine torque reactions in the frame and body to the minimum. PLYMOUTH uses two engine mountings at the rear but only one at the front.

V8 ENGINE

Chevrolet Superiorities

COMPLETELY NEW V8 ENGINE. CHEVROLET'S V8 engine is a completely new engine that was developed for use in CHEVROLET passenger cars. PLYMOUTH'S V8 engine is basically a Dodge truck engine that was revamped for passenger car use.

GREATER ACCELERATING POWER. CHEVROLET'S V8 engine develops 162 horsepower which is increased to 180 with CHEVROLET'S "power pack." PLYMOUTH'S original 1955 V8 engine developed less horsepower than the CHEVROLET, so PLYMOUTH increased the bore of their V8 to obtain a horsepower rating of 167. With the PLYMOUTH "power pack," this rebored engine develops only 177 horsepower. And the torque is only 231 foot-pounds, maximum, in either PLYMOUTH version whereas the CHEVROLET V8 maximum torque is 257 with standard equipment and 260 with the "power pack," giving CHEVROLET superior acceleration and hill-climbing ability.

SHORTER STROKE DESIGN. CHEVROLET'S large bore (3.75") and short stroke (3.0") provide a better oversquare design than PLYMOUTH'S smaller bore (3.56") and longer stroke (3.25")—resulting in less travel per mile for each piston and longer engine life.

LESS ENGINE WEIGHT. CHEVROLET'S compact and sturdy engine weighs only 488 pounds, whereas PLYMOUTH'S V8 weighs 575 pounds—87 more pounds that must be pulled.

HIGHER COMPRESSION RATIO. A higher compression ratio wrings more power from each drop of gasoline. The compression ratios for CHEVROLET and PLYMOUTH V8's are respectively 8.0 to 1 and 7.6 to 1.

CRANKSHAFT VIBRATION DAMPER. All CHEVROLET engines are equipped with a rubber-floated harmonic balancer which counteracts crankshaft vibration. The PLYMOUTH V8 crankshaft does not have a vibration damper.

PRESSED-IN PISTON PINS. CHEVROLET piston pins are solidly pressed in the connecting rod ends to prevent deflections of the upper ends of the connecting rods—thereby contributing to quieter engine operation and to greater engine durability. PLYMOUTH'S "floating type" piston pins tend to permit such deflections.

INDEPENDENT VALVE MECHANISMS. CHEVROLET'S exclusive separate valve trains provide quieter, more positive valve action at all speeds than PLYMOUTH'S conventional linkage.

BALL-BEARING WATER PUMP. A sealed, permanently-lubricated double-row ball bearing assures smooth operation of CHEVROLET'S water pump and engine fan. In PLYMOUTH'S water pump, a bushing, which tends to become ill-fitting and noisy, is used instead of an anti-friction bearing.

ENGINE FINAL-BALANCING. CHEVROLET'S scientific method of balancing the assembled engine, as well as its component parts, contributes to smoother and quieter engine operation. PLYMOUTH'S V8 engine is not balanced after assembly.

SMALLER OIL REQUIREMENTS. The CHEVROLET V8 requires one quart less oil every oil change than the PLYMOUTH V8. The respective oil refill capacities are four quarts and five quarts.

SMALLER ANTI-FREEZE REQUIREMENTS. CHEVROLET'S cooling system requires only 17 quarts of coolant (with heater) whereas PLYMOUTH'S requires 20 quarts.

"SIXES"

Chevrolet Superiorities

CHOICE OF *TWO* SIXES. CHEVROLET offers a choice of two six-cylinder engines: the "Blue-Flame 123" and the "Blue-Flame 136." PLYMOUTH provides one six.

GREATER POWER IN *BOTH* SIXES. The CHEVROLET "Blue-Flame 123," used with Synchro-mesh and Overdrive transmissions, is rated at 123 horsepower. The CHEVROLET "Blue-Flame 136," used with the automatic transmission, provides 136 horsepower. PLYMOUTH'S one six develops 117 horsepower, regardless of transmission choice.

GREATER TORQUE IN *BOTH* SIXES. Both CHEVROLET sixes provide better acceleration and hill-climbing ability because of their higher torque ratings: 209 ft. lb. for the "Blue-Flame 136" and 207 for the "Blue-Flame 123." The maximum torque of PLYMOUTH'S six is 194 foot pounds.

VALVE-IN-HEAD DESIGN. All CHEVROLET engines are the highly efficient, modern valve-in-head type, perfected through more than 40 years of experience with engines of this design. The PLYMOUTH Six is the L-head type, in which the valves are located in the cylinder block at the sides of the cylinders where they are subjected to more heat and are harder to service.

SHORTER STROKE. CHEVROLET'S stroke (both sixes) is only 3.94"; PLYMOUTH'S is 4.63." With a shorter stroke, pistons travel less per mile, contributing to longer engine life.

HIGHER COMPRESSION RATIO. Both of CHEVROLET'S six-cylinder engines have a compression ratio of 7.5 to 1, assuring better performance and gasoline economy than the 7.4 to 1 compression ratio of the PLYMOUTH Six.

OFFSET PISTON PINS. CHEVROLET'S piston pins are slightly off the center of the pistons to prevent piston slap. The piston pins of the PLYMOUTH Six are not offset.

LOCKED-IN-ROD PISTON PINS. CHEVROLET'S piston pins are solidly clamped in the connecting rod ends to prevent deflections of the upper ends of the connecting rods—thereby contributing to quieter engine operation and to greater engine durability. PLYMOUTH'S "floating type" piston pins tend to permit such deflections.

THREE PISTON RINGS. In the CHEVROLET sixes, only three piston rings per piston are necessary to assure proper oil sealing and engine compression. The PLYMOUTH Six requires four rings per piston.

HYDRAULIC VALVE LIFTERS. CHEVROLET provides self-adjusting hydraulic valve lifters in its "Blue-Flame 136" engine to assure a quieter, smoother valve operation with its quiet Powerglide automatic transmission. PLYMOUTH uses conventional mechanical valve lifters in its six, with or without the Powerflite automatic transmission.

WEDGE-SHAPED COMBUSTION CHAMBERS. CHEVROLET'S modern wedge-shaped chambers provide more efficient combustion for better engine performance and gasoline economy than can be obtained with the L-head cnambers of the PLYMOUTH Six.

CONCENTRIC CARBURETOR. The concentric carburetor used on both CHEVROLET sixes has twin floats that maintain a balanced fuel mixture even on curves or grades. The PLYMOUTH Six carburetor has just one float.

INTEGRAL VALVE SEATS. Because of CHEVROLET'S valve-in-head design, all valve seats are surrounded with water, assuring their proper cooling. PLYMOUTH exhaust valve seats, which are necessarily located near the hottest parts of the engine and cannot be surrounded with water, must be made of a special alloy to stand up under terrific engine heat.

WATER AROUND ALL CYLINDERS. Every CHEVROLET cylinder is completely surrounded by a full-length water jacket to assure uniform cooling of the cylinder walls, pistons, and rings. In the PLYMOUTH Six, the cylinders are "Siamesed" in pairs without any water space between the two cylinders of each pair.

BALL-BEARING WATER PUMP. A sealed, permanently-lubricated double-row ball bearing assures smooth operation of CHEVROLET'S water pump and engine fan. In PLYMOUTH'S water pump, a bushing, which tends to become ill-fitting and noisy, is used instead of an anti-friction bearing.

TRANSMISSIONS — STEERING — BRAKES

Chevrolet Superiorities

DIAPHRAGM SPRING CLUTCH. CHEVROLET'S simple diaphragm spring clutch always provides full facing contact, and the light pedal pressure required for its disengagement actually decreases as the pedal is pushed down. PLYMOUTH'S clutch, with its many coil springs and pressure levers, is a more complicated mechanism and requires increased pedal pressure as the engine speed increases.

WATER COOLING OF AUTOMATIC-TRANSMISSION OIL. PLYMOUTH'S automatic transmission still uses air cooling as compared to CHEVROLET'S more efficient controlled water cooling.

LEAKPROOF REAR AXLE. CHEVROLET'S new design and installation of rear wheel bearing seals makes the rear axle practically leakproof. PLYMOUTH'S method of installing their seals is the same as CHEVROLET discarded last year.

RECIRCULATING BALL-NUT STEERING GEAR. As in the most expensive cars, recirculating ball bearings in CHEVROLET'S steering gear reduce friction to the minimum to make steering smoother and easier and to make the steering gear more durable. PLYMOUTH still uses a worm and roller steering gear in its standard steering system.

EQUAL-LENGTH STEERING TIE RODS IN EVERY MODEL. For better balanced steering, CHEVROLET uses equal-length steering tie rods in every model. Although PLYMOUTH V8's also have this feature, every PLYMOUTH with a six-cylinder engine has tie rods of unequal lengths in its steering linkage.

LINKAGE-TYPE POWER STEERING. With the power cylinder built into the steering linkage, CHEVROLET'S optional power steering is quieter, easier to service and shock-free. PLYMOUTH'S coaxial-type power steering has the power cylinder integral with the steering gear, so that road-shock is transmitted into the steering column rather than into the chassis frame.

LARGER, SELF-ENERGIZING BRAKES. With CHEVROLET'S duo-servo brakes, all eight brake shoes (two at each wheel) are self-energizing whether the car is going forward or in reverse. In addition, all CHEVROLET brakes are eleven inches in diameter. Only six PLYMOUTH brake shoes are self-energizing in forward motion and only two are self-energizing in reverse motion. And PLYMOUTH'S brakes are only ten inches in diameter (except the front brakes on V8 models, which are eleven inches because of excessive engine weight, and eleven-inch rear brakes on V8 station wagons.)

DIRECT-ACTING PARKING BRAKES. Mechanical linkage connects the CHEVROLET hand brake control directly to the two enclosed rear wheel brakes to provide positive braking. In the PLYMOUTH, the hand brake control actuates a separate propeller shaft brake that is exposed to road dirt and splash.

BRAKING DIVE CONTROL. CHEVROLET'S braking dive control greatly reduces nose-diving of the car under all stopping conditions, assuring more comfortable stops and lessening the possibility of bumper locking and front end damage in case of sudden stops in close quarters. This feature is exclusive to CHEVROLET—in the industry.

In Summary . . .

The all-new Motoramic Chevrolet has a host
of valuable features that are not found in
either the Ford or Plymouth cars for 1955:

Polished lacquer finish • Body by Fisher • Unisteel body
construction with double-walled cowl, welded-in instrument
panel, center roof bow, and full double-walled body sides •
Mechanically attached door seals • Modern high-level
air intake • Optional Frigidaire air conditioner • Extra-
low-sill trunk • "Dip-down" belt line • Crank-regulated
ventipanes • Wraparound rear-quarter windows in station
wagons • Separate rear-quarter windows in four-door
sedans • Keyless door locking • One key for all car locks •
Automatic lock weather shields • Four-door automatic
interior-light switches* • Instrument panel interior-light
control • Automatic glove compartment light at no extra
cost** • Electric clock at no extra cost* • Concentric steering
column in all models • Cowl-arch-reinforced box-girder
frame • Sealed, plastic-lined spherical joints in the front
suspension • Recirculating-ball steering gear in all models •
Braking dive control • Outrigger rear suspension • Leakproof
rear axle • 12-volt electrical system • 54-plate battery
• Positive-shift starter • Four-point power plant mounting
• Diaphram spring clutch • Unique automatic transmission
features • and many other exclusive features in four of the
most modern V8's and Sixes in the industry!

PLUS

The most compact design for easiest maneuverability.
The heaviest basic car.
The best weight distribution.
The widest choice of high-compression power.
**The best combination of performance, economy, and
durability.**
The smallest turning circle and steepest ramp angles.
The most entrance room and head room.
The largest glass area—with the tallest windshield.
And the broadest-spaced, longest rear springs.

ALL IN THE LOWEST PRICED LINE
IN THE LOW-PRICE FIELD!

*In Bel Air models.   **In Bel Air and "Two Ten" models.

PRICES

Model for model, a Motoramic Chevrolet costs less to buy than a Ford or a Plymouth—as indicated by the *advertised delivered prices* of the three makes.

Advertised delivered prices, however, in every case are basic prices that are suggested by the manufacturer to the dealer. They include the suggested handling and delivery charges but, since they are quoted on an "F.O.B.—Factory" basis, necessarily do not include such charges as transportation costs and state and local taxes, which differ in each locality.

Therefore, the actual differences in costs between comparable models of the three competitive makes can be determined only through comparison of their *local delivered prices.*

To help Chevrolet salesmen to make such comparisons, the following charts list the comparable standard models of the three makes and their comparable optional equipment—with spaces in which the salesmen can write the *local delivered prices.*

RIVALS ANY CAR AT ANY COST!

V8 MODELS
LOCAL DELIVERED PRICES FOR COMPARABLE MODELS

	CHEVROLET	FORD	PLYMOUTH
4-DOOR SEDANS	"One-Fifty" 4-Door Sedan	Mainline Fordor	Plaza Four-Door Sedan
	"Two-Ten" 4-Door Sedan	Customline Fordor	Savoy Four-Door Sedan
	Bel Air 4-Door Sedan	Fairlane Town Sedan	Belvedere Four-Door Sedan
2-DOOR SEDANS	"One-Fifty" 2-Door Sedan	Mainline Tudor	Plaza Club Sedan
	"Two-Ten" 2-Door Sedan / "Two-Ten" Club Coupe	Customline Tudor	Savoy Club Sedan
	Bel Air 2-Door Sedan	Fairlane Club Sedan	Belvedere Club Sedan
SPORT COUPES	Bel Air Sport Coupe	Fairlane Victoria / Crown Victoria / Crown Victoria (with transparent top.)	Belvedere Sport Coupe

V8 MODELS

LOCAL DELIVERED PRICES FOR COMPARABLE MODELS

	CHEVROLET	FORD	PLYMOUTH
CONVERTIBLES	Bel Air Convertible	Fairlane Sunliner	Belvedere Convertible
BUSINESS COUPES	"One-Fifty" Utility Sedan	Mainline Business Sedan	Not Available
2-DOOR STATION WAGONS	"One-Fifty" Handyman	Ranch Wagon	Plaza Two-Door Suburban
2-DOOR STATION WAGONS	"Two-Ten" Handyman	Custom Ranch Wagon	Not Available
4-DOOR STATION WAGONS	"Two-Ten" Townsman	Country Sedan (6-pass.) (8-pass.)	Plaza* Four-Door Suburban
4-DOOR STATION WAGONS	Bel Air Beauville	Country Squire (8 pass.)	Belvedere Four-Door Suburban

*Lower-priced line; not directly comparable.

	CHEVROLET	FORD	PLYMOUTH
4-DOOR SEDANS	"One-Fifty" 4-Door Sedan	Mainline Fordor	Plaza Four-Door Seda
	"Two-Ten" 4-Door Sedan	Customline Fordor	Savoy Four-Door Seda
	Bel Air 4-Door Sedan	Fairlane Town Sedan	Belvedere Four-Door Seda
2-DOOR SEDANS	"One-Fifty" 2-Door Sedan	Mainline Tudor	Plaza Club Sedan
	"Two-Ten" 2-Door Sedan "Two-Ten" Club Coupe	Customline Tudor	Savoy Club Sedan
	Bel Air 2-Door Sedan	Fairlane Club Sedan	Belvedere Club Sedan
SPORT COUPES	Bel Air Sport Coupe	Fairlane Victoria Crown Victoria Crown Victoria (with transparent top)	Belvedere Sport Coupe

6-CYLINDER MODELS

LOCAL DELIVERED PRICES FOR COMPARABLE MODELS

	CHEVROLET	FORD	PLYMOUTH
CONVERTIBLES	Bel Air Convertible	Fairlane Sunliner	Not Available
BUSINESS COUPES	"One-Fifty" Utility Sedan	Mainline Business Sedan	Plaza Business Coupe
2-DOOR STATION WAGONS	"One-Fifty" Handyman	Ranch Wagon	Plaza Two-Door Suburban
2-DOOR STATION WAGONS	"Two-Ten" Handyman	Custom Ranch Wagon	Not Available
4-DOOR STATION WAGONS	"Two-Ten" Townsman	Country Sedan (6-pass.) (8-pass.)	Plaza* Four-Door Suburban
4-DOOR STATION WAGONS	Bel Air Beauville	Country Squire (8 pass.)	Belvedere Four-Door Suburban

*Lower-priced line; not directly comparable.

OPTIONAL EQUIPMENT

ITEM	CHEVROLET	FORD	PLYMOUTH
Automatic Transmission			
Overdrive			
Power Steering			
Power Brakes			
Power Pack (V8)			
Power Front Seat & Window Controls			
Heater, Outside Air			
Heater, Recirculating			
Air Conditioner			
Radio, Signal-Seeking		Not Available	Not Available
Radio, Pushbutton			
Radio, Manual		Not Available	Not Available
Direction Signals			
Tinted Glass			
Two-Tone Paint*			
White Sidewall Tires (added charge)			

*Not available on Ford Mainline models; standard on Plymouth Belvedere models.

INDEX

BOOK SECTION PAGE NUMBERS

The organization of this book necessitated that many of the Motoramic Chevrolet's features be mentioned in more than one of the book's sections. To help Chevrolet salesmen to identify the sections by their page numbers when looking up any item in the index, the page numbers for the various sections are listed here:

INDEX

Index

MEN OF CHEVROLET SALES

As all of you know, one of the greatest assets of any salesman is a thorough knowledge of his product. Enthusiasm, too, is an essential ingredient of good salesmanship but, to be fully convincing, it has to be backed up by solid facts and information. So a salesman not only has to be sold on his product—he also has to *know* it.

That's the purpose of this compact, pocket-sized data book—to help equip you with all the essential facts and information you need to know about the new Motoramic Chevrolet. We realize that with a product as complex as the luxurious modern-day car, no one can memorize each small detail. But here, in easy reference form, you will find all the car's important features described in detail and all the advantages comprehensively explained. Here, then, are all the facts to support your enthusiasm, and the information to meet the needs and questions of all your prospects and customers.

This book can serve you well, if you familiarize yourself with its contents and keep it as a ready reference. Together with your enthusiasm, energy and experience, it should help you sell more Motoramic Chevrolets—and carry you and Chevrolet to new heights of leadership in 1955.

W. E. Fish

General Sales Manager